Miss Jacqueline Christeve
40 Lily Way
Watsonville, CA 95076

THE HEALING CONNECTION

Also by Jean Baker Miller and Irene Pierce Stiver:

WOMEN'S GROWTH IN CONNECTION
(written with Judith Jordan, Alexandra Kaplan, and Janet S. Surrey)

Also by Jean Baker Miller:

TOWARD A NEW PSYCHOLOGY OF WOMEN

PSYCHOANALYSIS AND WOMEN (editor)

Jean Baker Miller, M.D.

THE HEALING

HOW WOMEN FORM RELATIONSHIPS IN THERAPY AND IN LIFE

CONNECTION

Irene Pierce Stiver, Ph.D.

Beacon Press

Boston

Beacon Press
25 Beacon Street
Boston, Massachusetts 02108-2892

Beacon Press Books are published under the auspices of
the Unitarian Universalist Association of Congregations.

Printed in the United States of America

02   01   00   99   98   97   8   7   6   5   4   3   2   1

Text design by Julia Sedykh
Composition by Wilsted & Taylor Publishing Services

Library of Congress Cataloging-in-Publication Data
Miller, Jean Baker.
The healing connection: how women form relationships in therapy and in life /
Jean Baker Miller and Irene Pierce Stiver.
p. cm.
Includes bibliographical references and index.
ISBN 0-8070-2920-3
1. Women—Mental health.   2. Interpersonal relations.   3. Empathy.   4. Women—
Psychology.   5. Alienation (Social psychology)   6. Psychotherapist and patient.
I. Stiver, Irene P.   II. Title.
RC451.4.W6M57   1997
155.6'33—dc21   97-14151

TO

Ray and Lynne

Mike, Ned, Jon, Myriam, and Jake

CONTENTS

ACKNOWLEDGMENTS

With great warmth and affection we express our special appreciation to Judith Jordan and Janet Surrey. We four are members of a core group that has been meeting for twenty years to work on the development of a better understanding of the psychology of women — and ultimately, of all human beings.

The ideas presented here grow out of our common endeavors and represent just one branch of the basic work we have done together over the years. It has been a unique experience, full of zest, hard work, and fun, to work closely with such friends and colleagues. We are deeply grateful to them. We will describe their work further in the introduction and throughout this book.

In addition to this core group, we want to thank a larger number of students, supervisees, and colleagues from whom we have learned. In recent years they have included Diane Becker, Steve Bergman, Mary Collins, Robin Cook-Nobles, Mimi Dohan, Catherine Dooley, Susan Eaton, Natalie Eldridge, Denise Elliott, Niki Fedele, Susan Filene, Joyce Fletcher, Nancy Gleason, Elizabeth Harrington, Maureen Harvey, Judith Herman, Andrea Johnson, Yvonne Jenkins, Kay Kahn, Alexandra Kaplan, Lori Kaplowitz, Carol Kauffman, Marisa Laviola, Lynne Lieberman, Diane Littlefield, Jane MacDonald, Julie Mencher, Susan Miller, Marsha Pravda Mirkin, Pamela Peck, Wendy Rosen, Barbara Rosenthal, Julie Ross, Georgia Sassen, Barbara Schwartz, Suzanne Slater, Carolyn Swift, Beverly Daniel Tatum, Maureen Walker, and Laura Woodburn. We've also learned from women all over the country (and some in other countries) who have attended sessions where we have spoken and who continue to interact with us. Many have established study groups, which has led to their conducting teaching conferences in their areas, developing research projects, and exploring the wider applications of our work.

Our close colleagues Judith Jordan and Janet Surrey have read this manuscript and made major contributions to it, as they have to all of our work together. For a long time now, Carol Gilligan's work has played a special part in our endeavors. We have been traveling a similar although not identical road, pursuing new conceptions and questioning old formulations. We believe this work leads to a whole new view of psychology and opens up an enlarged vision of all of life. In doing so, it also offers a new basis for work in many fields beyond psychology. Carol and we have found great pleasure in discovering that our work often confirmed each other's thinking. Further, we are grateful to her for reading a large part of this manuscript and giving us her insightful suggestions. Christina Robb has also read large portions of this manuscript and has been a most enthusiastic and astute advisor. Her depth of understanding and knowledge has been a valuable gift to us.

We owe a particular and unique debt to our patients. Many of them are represented in this book. In all instances they have been heavily disguised to protect their privacy, but we hope that we have been able to portray the essence of our work together. They have made it possible for us to create with them the growth-fostering new experience that psychotherapy can be.

We are grateful to the Stone Center for Developmental Services and Studies at Wellesley College, now a part of the Wellesley Centers for Women, and to the center's staff and overseers, with whom we have worked for many years. Several of the center's directors have been most supportive of our work, including Carolyn Swift, Maud Chaplin, Cynthia García Coll, Joanne Murray, and Susan Bailey. Janet Rubenstein has been a devoted assistant and has helped to carry forward many programs and projects.

We have also relied on a great deal of help from several writers and editors. MaryAnn Lash has been with us throughout; her encouragement and her talent have sustained us and have had a profound effect on the whole book. We are very grateful to Lauren Bryant, who advised us on the book and also rewrote a significant part of the first chapter. Marya E. Van't Hul of Beacon Press has been a delight to work with. She has been most encouraging and empowering. Her excellent ideas and critique have improved this book immensely. Moreover, she helped to translate this book into much greater clarity. With great energy, our agent, Anne Borchardt, has applied her extensive literary expertise to bringing this book into existence.

We count ourselves as incredibly fortunate to have husbands who take pleasure in our work — S. M. (Mike) Miller and Ray Stiver. Characteristically, they have enjoyed the exploration of our ideas with us. They too have read this manuscript and given us invaluable comments and suggestions, and they have been supportive and dedicated beyond measure in many other ways, large and small; they have enriched our lives with their warmth, generosity, and good humor. Other people who have brought us help and joy, along with good ideas, are Irene's niece, Lynne Lieberman; Jean's sons, Edward D. (Ned) and Jon; and Jean's daughter-in-law, Myriam Barenbaum, and grandson, Jake.

INTRODUCTION

During the late sixties and early seventies, feminist writers began to show that traditional psychodynamic theories and forms of practice neglected or misunderstood many aspects of women's experience. Their work inspired us and our colleagues Judith Jordan and Janet Surrey to think about these issues more systematically. We began in 1977 to meet in our "Monday Night Group" and this book is a product of that group. It emerges out of the exchanges we have created together. At times our ideas flowed from the interactions among us, so that it would be inappropriate to say that any idea "belonged" to any one person; each idea became enlarged and transformed in interchange, was not what it was when it began, and is truly everyone's creation. Thus, this book represents all of us.

We are all clinicians with many years' experience who came together to try to better understand women's psychological development, the problems women encounter, and what to do about them. Our work grows out of this clinical background; all of us were trained in, and practiced, one or another form of psychodynamic psychotherapy.

We began by closely examining the experience of the women with whom we work. The more we examined, the more we found that traditional explanations could not suffice; and the more these explanations did not suffice, the more we realized that certain of the basic premises behind them could not hold up.

All psychological formulations rest on an underlying theory and set of assumptions although these are not always made explicit. This holds true for both popular and professional literature. When the underlying theory is not explicit, most formulations tend to accept the prevalent thinking in the field, which in turn usually reflects dominant cultural assumptions. Underlying theory can be difficult to identify; it is ubiquitous and, like all cultural assumptions, can seem "natural" or self-evident.

As formally trained therapists, we were all strongly influenced by traditional psychoanalytic concepts, concepts that reflect societal and cultural assumptions so deeply entrenched in all of us that we scarcely question their validity, we simply think of them as "the truth" about human development. For instance, psychoanalytic thinking has taken over without question the Western notion that becoming a self-sufficient individual is the goal of human psychological development. Our society has in turn readily taken up the psychoanalytic idea that a great many psychological (and social) problems have their origins in the early mother-infant relationship, specifically in the mother's failure to allow the child to become fully independent and self-sufficient.

The notion of separation as a goal has become the standard by which, we are told, we should define our ourselves as healthy human beings. Independence and self-sufficiency are considered the hallmarks of maturity; the key process in psychological development is said to be the growth of an inner sense of separation and individuation. Thus, for instance, we learn that children must begin very early to separate from their parents, especially their mothers, in order to move successfully into adolescence and adulthood; adolescents must emotionally and psychologically separate from their parents to fulfill their own needs and grow.

But our experience has led us to a different emphasis for understanding psychological development. This book is about connections between people, about how we create them and how disconnections derail them throughout our lives. Just as disconnections restrict us and block psychological growth, connections — the experience of mutual engagement and empathy — provide the original and continuing sources of that growth. This book is also about our belief that an understanding of the powerful role of connections in human growth alters the entire basis of contemporary psychological theory and psychotherapy. As such, it reflects a major shift in our thinking about what creates pain and psychological problems and what fosters healing and growth. Most important, this book is about how the making of connections can transform all the institutions in our lives, from school to workplace to home.

Throughout this book, we will elaborate on what we mean by connections and disconnections. We will explore why relationships in our culture so often lead to the roadblocks of disconnection — to anxiety, isolation, and depression. And we will strive to make evident how these roadblocks can be turned into pathways of connection. We will explain, too, how connection, not separation, leads to strong, healthy people.

Although our work in the Monday Night Group and with other colleagues has focused on women, we have come to believe that the new premises we have arrived at lead us on to a new way of viewing all human development and its derailments. By trying to explore more deeply the parts of life that have been assigned to women traditionally, we discover aspects of everyone's life that have been neglected and devalued. Understanding and reframing these parts of life create a different picture for both women and men — it gives us a vision of how living can be transformed for all people. Thus in this book we will speak mainly about women, but we will point to the implications of this vision for everyone.

———

Since our work together began in 1977, we have been joined by a number of other people. In 1981, Alexandra Kaplan joined the Monday Night Group for several years until she became ill some years ago. In that year we also became associated with the Stone Center at Wellesley College. The center is dedicated to the prevention of psychological problems, the enhancement of psychological development, and the search for a more comprehensive understanding of human development. It seeks to pay particular attention to the experiences of women, children, and families across culturally diverse populations. Its mission is carried out through education, research, and community outreach.

At the Stone Center we have participated in a number of research and action programs based on the ideas we have been developing, including an educational program. Over the years the latter has included many presentations, workshops, seminars, and conferences and we (the authors and Judith Jordan and Janet Surrey) became known as "the theory group."[1] As a part of these research and educational endeavors many more people have joined us in this work. Thus our book also draws upon the contributions of a great many people throughout this country and abroad who have enlarged our understanding. The work covers numerous areas of psychological development, psychological problems, and various methods of treatment based on a relational model organized around the importance of growth-fostering connections in relationships. Much of it has been reported in the Stone Center Working Paper series and Project Reports, which number over eighty.[2] The early core working papers have been collected into a volume, *Women's Growth in Connection;* a second collection, *Women's Growth in Diversity*, was published in 1997.[3]

We are pleased to say that women of diverse cultural backgrounds are now creating an increasing proportion of this work. We recognize our own limitations in that much of our own experience has been with white women, albeit not all of them from the middle class. Therefore, we can still speak only from this partial perspective.

For a long time now, our group has had a strong commitment to demystifying psychological and psychotherapeutic language. We believe that the language commonly used in the field is not only mystifying but pejorative, denigrating, and distancing. Much of the subject matter it refers to is complex, but we believe that these topics can be discussed in more ordinary language. (This is a continuing struggle for us, and we ourselves may still fall into bad habits of language.)

We are clinicians, and most of what we have to say in this book grows out of our practice with people, some of it enlarged by psychological research. We have each been practicing for over forty years; Irene has taught psychology and psychotherapy for forty-five years, and Jean psychiatry and psychotherapy for thirty-six years. Though this may seem a limited perspective for proposing sweeping changes in the world, as we do in this book, we still want to make these proposals.

Clinical work allows us the privilege of sharing what really goes on in people's lives. We see what living in this world does to people and we think we see why. We also see how people can change and grow, and we see a way to a different kind of living. We believe this path emerges from an understanding of certain parts of the human potential that are essential and already exist in this world but have been suppressed and devalued. We believe that they can be brought to light and to life; however, in coming to full life they also have to be transformed. In this book we try to describe how this can happen.

We also describe how this understanding changes the way we do therapy. Our reframing of therapy centers around creating a new relationship in which both therapist and patient can form a connection that is authentic and growth-fostering for both people. In such a setting, patients can begin to represent themselves more fully and then bring more of themselves into other relationships in their lives and in the world.[4]

We hope that this book will provide some glimpses of how this relational approach can lead to changes in the larger world, and that others will see ways to extend this work.

PART ONE

CONNECTIONS

——

RELATIONSHIPS REVISITED

━━

We begin with a set of stories that offer examples of significant moments in common relationships.

Susan, who is in her late thirties, is about to visit her father in the hospital. He is eighty years old and seriously ill. Susan is one of her father's few remaining relatives, and she is concerned over his failing health, but she lives 1,800 miles away, and has found it hard to make arrangements to visit him regularly. She and her father have had a difficult relationship over the years; he was often critical of her, expressing disappointment, for instance, over her choices of job and husband. Susan has not often felt close to her father, but on this occasion she has made a special effort to be with him — paying an expensive plane fare and juggling her job responsibilities, her two school-age children's schedules, and her husband's needs. Before going to the hospital, she goes out of her way to find a box of the special cookies she knows her father likes. Susan is eager to talk with her father, though she dreads seeing him ill and unhappy.

When Susan arrives at the hospital she is shocked by how fragile her father looks, but she puts on a cheerful demeanor and greets him enthusiastically as she hands him the cookies. He takes the box, hurls it across the bed, and says angrily, "Don't you know I can't eat these anymore?!" Susan is mortified and tells herself she should have realized about the cookies. She recognizes that her father is irritable because he is ill and tries to think of other ways to cheer him up, but she finds herself growing increasingly silent for the rest of the visit, at a loss for what to say or do next.

What happened between Susan and her father? Susan had wanted the visit to go well and to get closer to her aging father. But in the end, she and her father are both upset and just as far apart as ever. A similar gulf exists in the next story, between Debbie and her mother.

Debbie, a high school junior, bursts through the door of her house after school and tells her mother that her boyfriend of six months has just broken up with her so he can date other people. Debbie is distraught and weeping. Through her tears, she tells her mother that she feels ugly, that she hates her former boyfriend, that she also loves him, that she wants to die. Debbie's mother, who had not been very fond of the boyfriend, is relieved that the relationship is over, but she is disturbed to see her daughter so obviously heartbroken and unhappy. Debbie is inconsolable as her mother tries to cheer her by telling her how pretty she is and how she will attract new boyfriends. She also tells Debbie that she never really liked the boyfriend but didn't say anything while they were dating because Debbie cared for him so much. The more her mother talks, the more upset Debbie becomes. "You don't understand!" she screams. "Leave me alone! I don't want to talk to you! You don't understand anything!" Debbie withdraws and refuses to talk to her mother at all. Debbie is miserable and her mother feels terrible.

How have Debbie and her mother reached this impasse? Clearly,

Debbie was seeking comfort from her mother, and just as clearly, her mother thought that she could reassure her daughter and ease her pain. Yet the more her mother tried to help Debbie "get over it," the more antagonistic their relationship became. Such a dissonance also arises in our third story, between Claudia and Lydia, two women who work together in the same office.

Claudia and Lydia, two secretaries, work for the same boss. They take pride in the fact that they work for a person who occupies one of the most powerful positions in the company. They are also pleased that they manage to work well together, despite their boss's reputation for being demanding and unpredictable, and the high pressure of their work environment.

One day Claudia returns to the office she shares with Lydia after a meeting with their boss. She is in tears and has a difficult time telling Lydia what has happened. Haltingly, she tells Lydia that the boss has exploded about a project Claudia was working on, criticizing most of what she has done. Lydia interrupts, reminding Claudia that it's their boss's manner to be critical and contemptuous. Claudia says that this time she feels particularly stupid and undervalued. Lydia responds with irritation: "How could you let him talk to you that way? You should stand up for yourself. I would never give him the satisfaction of seeing me cry." Claudia grows even more distressed and flees the office quickly, feeling even more inadequate.

What happened between these two friends that caused divisiveness? Why was Lydia unable to empathize with Claudia's distress?

Each of these stories ends abruptly with a critical *disconnection*, a moment when the people involved experience the pain of not being understood and of not understanding the other person. Disconnections are what we experience when we feel cut off from those with whom we share a relationship.

To begin to better understand how disconnections occur, let us briefly imagine our three stories with some key differences.

What if Susan had not fallen silent but had said, "Dad, I really wanted this to be a good visit. I know you feel bad and I wanted to cheer you up. But whenever I try to show you that I care, you do something that makes me feel awful"? What if Susan's father had been able to express his feelings about being ill, and about seeing his daughter again for what might be the last time?

What if Debbie's mother had set aside her own anxiety over her daughter's unhappiness and said, "I may know how awful you feel. I had an experience like this once, and it was terrible"? What if she was also able to admit to Debbie that it was painful to see her so sad? What if Debbie had spoken up and told her mother that it hurt to have her feelings minimized, that what she really needed was her mother's understanding?

What if Lydia had acknowledged Claudia's humiliation and admitted that she had felt it too? What if Claudia had responded to Lydia's irritation by telling her that the pep talk only made her feel worse? What if Lydia and Claudia had taken the opportunity to talk about how they could work together to find ways of countering the power their boss held over them?

If any one of these "what ifs" had occurred, a painful moment of disconnection might have been transformed into a powerful moment of connection. But we all know how extraordinarily hard it can sometimes be to connect with another person, and this is especially true when there are differences in power between individuals within a relationship.

We all live in a world in which some people, or groups of people, hold power over others based on differences in age, race, class, gender, sexual orientation, or other factors. When power inequities — whether real or assumed — are present, disconnections can readily occur. Furthermore, the experience of growing up and living within such a "power-over" framework influences all of our actions, even in the most personal situations and even when there is no power differential present.

For both Susan and Debbie, a history of power inequities and the disconnections caused by power-over relationships pervades their thinking, permeates their feelings, and restricts their vision of what changes might be possible in their significant relationships. Even the relationship between Claudia and Lydia, two equals, is seriously affected by the power-over context in which they work.

———

These notions about connections, disconnections, and power move us away from traditional psychological concerns. To illustrate the kind of encounter that has led us to explore another path, we will relate a story from clinical experience.

Some time ago, Irene was responsible for supervising a psychology trainee at McLean Hospital, near Boston. This trainee, a woman, held an initial interview with a young working-class woman we'll call Jane. Jane reported that she wanted therapy to help her with recent difficulties in concentrating and the subsequent problems she was having at her job. She thought her problems had something to do with the death of her mother, with whom she had been very close, over a year before. As the trainee explored Jane's thoughts about her mother's death, Jane became increasingly distraught and tearful. The trainee was very moved by Jane's story. At the end of the hour Jane asked if it would be possible for her to come to therapy twice a week.

In Irene's initial supervisory meeting with the trainee, she praised her interaction with Jane. In Irene's view, Jane's request for two therapy sessions a week reflected how sensitive and responsive the trainee had been.

As part of her educational program, the trainee also presented this interview to a team headed by a male psychoanalyst. He was concerned with what he felt was an "escalation of affect" (that is, of emotion) in the interview, which he believed suggested that Jane was a "hysterical personality," easily "stimulated" to express intense emotions. He criticized the trainee for being "too seductive" in encouraging Jane to "pour out" her feelings and to "depend too much" on the trainee. He saw Jane as an overly dependent person whose dependency needs should be discouraged; rather than seeing Jane twice a week, which according to him would only intensify her "neediness" or even lead to a "regression" to childish behavior, he recommended that the trainee see Jane only every other week, to set limits on her "demandingness." Finally, he speculated on the meanings of Jane's intense feelings about her mother; he wondered whether her difficulties in separating from her mother may have resulted in an "enmeshed" relationship, which contributed to her difficulties in adjusting to her mother's death.

Irene was very troubled by this evaluation. To Irene, Jane did not seem overly dependent, rather she seemed impressive in her ability to connect with the trainee so quickly, as well as genuinely caring in her relationships with colleagues and friends. Jane's sadness over her mother's death seemed appropriate to the significant loss she had experienced. While not unmindful of the complexities of the mother-daughter relationship, Irene and her trainee thought that for Jane therapy twice a week was a good idea.

Irene brought Jane's story to our "Monday Night Group," the group of female colleagues we describe in the introduction. At the time we were using our meetings to examine differences between our own understandings of the women we were treating and the traditional clinical perspectives that surrounded us. When we listened carefully to what Jane had said, it became clear that her sadness had little to do with being enmeshed or too dependent. Rather, she was suffering from the loss of a critical connection in her life.

Our observations about Jane matched certain conclusions we had reached about other women's stories we had discussed together. We had begun to see how frequently women patients were labeled as being hysterical when they expressed strong emotions. In Jane's story we saw yet another instance in which a woman's experience was pathologized; what we saw as women's valid close connections to others were frequently dismissed as "masochistic," "dependent," or "engulfing" by a mental health profession dominated by male views of development. Independence, controlled emotional expression, and separation — particularly from one's mother — were considered signs of psychological health.

Our group discussions enabled all of us to be more confident in challenging typical traditional psychological assessments of the women we encountered. Rather than labeling Jane's relationship with her mother problematic, Irene urged her trainee to honor that connection. Over time, Jane progressed very well on two therapy sessions a week. Dependency never became an issue in these sessions. What the analyst had seen as dependency between the trainee and Jane was, in our view, the trainee's appropriate expression of caring and Jane's response to this caring. In fact, as her therapy came to an end, Jane reported that what had helped her most was her therapist's responsiveness to her strong feelings.

In the view of standard theory, then, Jane was seen as not having achieved the required separation from her mother; thus she was considered overly dependent and unable to cope with life's problems on her own. Our experience with Jane, and hundreds of other women whom we have met over the years, has led us away from this view, toward a profound shift in our fundamental understanding of human psychological development. It has not been an easy shift to make.

We were moving away from certain basic assumptions of both professional and popular wisdom. A glance at contemporary bookstore shelves confirms how widely accepted these assumptions are. A veritable industry has emerged in recent years to produce and promote books that urge women to separate, to become independent. Women "love too much," they are "addicted to relationships," or, to quote an earlier pop phrase, they suffer from a "Cinderella complex" (that is, they want to be saved by a man). If a women remains strongly connected — to her mother, her family, her spouse or partner — she is deemed dependent. She must "grow beyond dependence" in order to thrive. In short, these books often blame women for not "doing it right" (for choosing the wrong men, for being codependent, etc.).

But the fact is, women do do it right in many ways. The fault lies elsewhere, as we hope to demonstrate.

Many popular psychology books suffer from a central problem: like traditional psychoanalytic theories, they rest on a limited understanding of women's lives. They aim to offer new possibilities and opportunities for women's growth, but their interpretations rely on an old framework of unquestioned assumptions about the value of separation and autonomy. While some of these books have helped some women (ironically, often by helping them feel less alone and more connected to others), at bottom they pathologize women's actual experience.

If we observe women's lives carefully, without attempting to force our observations into preexisting patterns, we discover that an inner sense of connection to others is *the* central organizing feature of women's development. By listening to the stories women tell about their lives and examining these stories seriously, we have found that, quite contrary to what one would expect based on the governing models of development emphasizing separation, women's sense of self and of worth is most often grounded in the ability to make and maintain relationships. As Jean wrote in her book *Toward a New Psychology of Women* (1976), "Women stay with, build on, and develop in a context of connections with others."[1]

If we explore the context of connections in which they function, we find a central concern in the lives of most women that can be described as "the active participation in the development of other people," certainly in the development of children but also in that of adults.[2] To define this participation more clearly, let us stress first what it is not. It is not simply "nurturing," "serving others," a "maternal instinct," or the ability to "fulfill others' needs." These words do not adequately describe the complex activity involved when a person engages others in such a manner as to foster their psychological development. While words like "nurturing" and the like may convey a part of what it means to participate in this way in relationships with others, our language does not yet contain a word or phrase that captures the fullness of this activity. We call it participating in growth-fostering relationships.

Such phrases sound strange. They are. We are trying to name a basic human activity that has not been well recognized or described in ways that portray its importance, complexity, and creativity. But it is activity that is going on all the time. Another word we use in discussing this kind of participation in relationships — power — may sound even stranger at first; yet an individual can exert enormous power in the role of fostering the growth of others: "Women use their power . . . to increase the other person's resources and strengths in many dimensions — emotional, intellectual, psychological, and more."[3] This is not a power over others, directing and controlling them; it is "power with," a power that grows as it is used to empower others.

Of course, no human develops in isolation; most theorists have long agreed that people develop only in interaction with others. But in these interactions all of us are always either participating in ways that foster the growth of a relationship and the people involved in it, or we are not participating in growth-fostering ways.

To talk of participating in others' psychological development, then, is to talk about a form of activity that is essential to human life. In general, our society has assigned this fundamental activity — and the distinctive knowledge it entails — to women. It is significant that this knowledge had long been ignored in our psychological theories and demeaned in our larger culture, yet it is from this perspective that a new vision of psychological and emotional health for all people may be glimpsed. In reclaiming the knowledge about relationships that women in particular hold, we can begin to form a new model of psychological development *within relationships*, in which everyone participates in ways that foster the development of all the people involved, something we might call "mutual psychological development." This vision of mutual development includes not only individuals and families, but also workplaces, schools, and other institutions — in other words, all of life.

We do not mean to falsely idealize women. We do not believe that a knowledge of how to create and sustain growth-fostering relationships has to be limited by gender. Nor do we think that this knowledge is linked to something innate or biological. Certainly individual women can be coercive, destructive, or abusive, exhibiting the most violating aspects of power-over relationships with others. We also recognize that many women may find it impossible to develop mutually empathic relationships in a society that sees qualities such as empathy as deficiencies and is characterized by so much woman- and mother-blaming. As a general fact, though, in our culture it is women who have long done much of the work of building growth-fostering relationships for the society as a whole, and so we believe that it is from women's lives and experience that we can best learn about the potential power of a relational approach toward all of human development.

When we talk of women, we recognize that we have the expertise to talk only about women in the current dominant white culture in the United States. We do not mean to imply that all women in all times and places are covered by our generalizations. We know that within our own society there are variations among women, especially on the bases of race, ethnicity, class, and sexual preference. We would like to suggest, however, that our general propositions may be relevant. Significant additions and alterations must be added in talking of women of marginalized groups. As described in the introduction, members of several Stone Center study groups are working on the possible integration of the relational approach with the experience of marginalized groups.[4]

An eloquent example of the power of a mutually growth-fostering relationship exists in the following exchange between two women friends, Rachel Carson, the author of *Silent Spring*, and her summer neighbor in Maine, Dorothy Freeman. In 1953, Carson, already a very successful writer, and Freeman, who lived most of the time with her husband in Massachusetts, began a correspondence that would flourish over the next dozen years. Early in 1954, Carson wrote to her friend:

> All I am certain of is this; that it is quite necessary for me to know that there is someone who is deeply devoted to me as a person, and who also has the capacity and the depth of understanding to share, vicariously, the crushing burden of creative effort, recognizing the heartache, the great weariness of mind and body, the occasional black depair it may involve — someone who cherishes me and what I am trying to create, as well. Last summer I was feeling as never before, that there was no one who combined all of that. . . . And then . . . you came into my life! . . . Very early in our correspondence last fall I began to sense that capacity to enter so fully into the intellectual and creative parts of my life as well as to be a dearly loved friend.

Years later, Freeman wrote to Carson about that 1954 letter, which had come to represent something central to their relationship.

> I have read again [the 1954 letter]. How very, very precious it is. . . . Can you *now*, did you *ever* understand what all that meant

to me? Remember that then you were the Famous Author, on a pedestal, with that gulf between us. In that letter the gulf was bridged . . . altho' it took a long time to destroy that pedestal. Its destruction came when I grew to know you as a person who had worldly cares and burdens and heartaches as I had.

. . . In the going-on-eight years in which I've known you, my life has been enriched, broadened, sweetened, smoothed, softened, and enlarged beyond expressing.[5]

While these letters contain the words of two very eloquent women, they also express an experience vital to us all — the necessity of being heard and understood as well as hearing and understanding another.

Our point about women's way of being may sound familiar, especially to those who follow the field of women's psychology. The vision of mutually growth-fostering relationships we hold in this book emerges from earlier work that has also taken women's lives as a starting point. Over the last three decades, women writers have created an extensive body of work about women's experience. In the field of psychology, these writings can be divided into two groups. Some writers have worked on modifications of existing formulations such as Freudian, Jungian, or object relations theories. Others — and we count ourselves among this group — have proposed that the close study of women's experience leads to the creation of new frameworks based on new assumptions.

Jean was among the very first writers in our field to observe that women's relational strengths have typically been demeaned as weaknesses, devalued by a mental health profession that echoes the surrounding patriarchal culture. With its insistence that women's specific life experiences must be the starting point from which to understand women's psychology, *Toward a New Psychology of Women* challenged major assumptions that had long guided standard theories of psychological development. It also laid the groundwork for the analysis of connections carried out in this book. As Jean put it then,

In many ways, women have "filled in" [the essential activities of caring for and fostering human growth] all along. Precisely be-

cause they have done so, women have developed the foundations
of extremely valuable psychological qualities, which we are only
beginning to understand. I hope that soon knowledge gained
from several areas of study will help us to delineate these
strengths and their dynamic operation in richer and more pre-
cise terms.[6]

The papers in *Women's Growth in Connection*, by all the members of
our Monday Night Group, and other Stone Center Working Papers
explicate further the ideas that led us to this book.[7]

An early paper by Carol Gilligan, and the book that followed, *In
a Different Voice* (1982), attended specifically to women's experience.[8] Previous research on moral development had concluded that
boys and men reach higher levels of moral development than girls
and women. Gilligan noted, however, that the standards by which
moral development was evaluated were based on responses of boys
and men only; women were not represented at all in the process of
establishing these standards. As she listened to women in her own
study, Gilligan heard how often the responses of women, when
making choices or in situations of conflict, were informed by a relational perspective and a complex appreciation of context, yet their
decisions — their "voices" — were heard as deficient and underde-
veloped in the existing research. Gilligan's incisive findings led her
on to ask new questions and to open up a different perspective on
what had been a limited notion of psychological development.
Since then, Gilligan and her group have explored this relational approach in a variety of contexts.[9]

The present book has roots in Jean's earlier work and owes a large
debt to the research of Carol Gilligan. We have benefited as well
from the work of sociologist Nancy Chodorow, whose book *The
Reproduction of Mothering* (1978) offered an analysis of gender
differences within the context of psychoanalytic object relations
theory. Chodorow noted that when growing up, little girls were not
encouraged toward separate strivings nor were they pushed to
achieve a separate identity from their mothers in the way that little
boys were. In doing this work, however, she did not move beyond
traditional psychoanalytic assumptions.[10] The work of Mary Be-

lenky, Blythe Clinchy, Nancy Goldberger, and Jill Tarule in their book *Women's Way of Knowing: The Development of Self, Voice, and Mind* (1986) extended a relational approach to cognitive development by exploring how women's relational way of being is linked to their thinking and learning, thereby creating an enlarged conception of what thinking and learning are.[11] And there have been many other women in a variety of fields, such as Phyllis Chesler, Audre Lorde, and Adrienne Rich, from whom we have learned an enormous amount.[12]

In the present book we are not talking about the question of sex or gender differences *per se*. Our concern is not how different, or how similar, men and women are. Instead, we have set out to accurately describe women's experience — a still-neglected realm — so as to highlight the fact that certain psychological activities that are vital to the health of all human beings occur in growth-fostering relationships.

For brevity we call our endeavor a relational approach to understanding psychological development and psychotherapy. (It would be more accurate to call it a growth-fostering relational approach, but that phrase is too cumbersome.) However, we depart from the relational approaches to psychodynamics and psychotherapy that a number of other writers have been developing since we have been working on our model. While we have learned a great deal from earlier relational theorists,[13] and also from the recent work of "self psychologists," the relational theorists at New York University's Postdoctoral Program in Psychotherapy and Psychoanalysis, and Robert Stolorow and his associates,[14] and others, our work has some major differences.

Most importantly, these writers do not emphasize how our culture influences relationships in general in negative ways, or how relationships might change if approached from a view arising out of women's experience. In particular, they do not take into account the issue of differences of power, nor has their work evolved from an analysis of gender. This last point is particularly important since it can be argued that women have been the "carriers" of relationships for our culture. Even though these theorists emphasize the importance of relationships in an individual's psychological development, they have not paid sufficient attention to the very people who, for the most part, create and sustain growth-fostering relationships. At root, these theorists retain the basic notion that relationships are the means to the development of the separate self.

In our view, the goal of development is not forming a separated self or finding gratification, but something else altogether — the ability to participate actively in relationships that foster the well-being of everyone involved. Our fundamental notions of who we are are not formed in the process of separation from others, but within the mutual interplay of relationships with others. In short, the goal is not for the individual to grow out of relationships, but to grow into them. As the relationships grow, so grows the individual. Participating in growth-fostering relationships is both the source and the goal of development.

In sum, our book seeks to go beyond earlier approaches. A full-fledged theory of women's psychological development does not yet exist; our work pursues that goal. Moreover, we believe that the insights we have gleaned from women's experience about how growth-fostering relationships can be created, or stymied, are relevant not only to theories of women's psychological development but to the human condition in general.

We have outlined some bold claims that need to be explained. In the chapters to come, we will look closely at the definition and implications of connections, disconnections, and relationships, relying upon examples gathered from our individual practices and on our work at the Stone Center at Wellesley College and elsewhere.

Our focus on the significance of disconnections and connections has led us to interact differently with the people we treat. Instead of stressing the importance of the therapist's neutrality, we believe the therapist must be authentically present and participating in the therapy relationship. We will illustrate this change with examples from our practices.

Therapy is only one kind of relationship that can be revolutionized by an understanding of how disconnections and connections work. We believe all of our relationships — in families, workplaces, and schools; between parent and child, sibling and sibling, teacher and student, colleague and colleague — can be renewed by restoring the pathways to connection. As we move into authentic connections with the people in our lives, we will find more common ground with them, leading us toward an enlarged sense of community and of possibilities for social change. Making connections has implications for the world, not only for our individual lives.

Before moving on, we want to state one major caveat. We will be talking in the next chapter and in other places about optimal human connections. These are ideal types that we set forth in order to explain a theory. In reality, most of us struggle with various mixtures of connection and disconnection. We hope to explain why, but we are not intending to propose yet another impossible standard for judging women — or men.

2

HOW DO CONNECTIONS
LEAD TO GROWTH?

━━

What kinds of relationships lead to the growth of the people in them — that is, to psychological development? What kinds of relationships diminish or destroy people — lead to psychological trouble or eventually to what is called psychopathology? We'll begin to address these questions by looking closely at how two interactions about the same event might go.

Ann, a twenty-five-year-old factory worker, has just heard from her friend and coworker Emily that Emily may have a serious disease. Ann is telling a mutual friend, Beth, about this. Tears well up in Ann's eyes, and her voice sounds sad and fearful. "Oh, how sad," Beth says. Her voice and expression also convey sadness as well as fear. "Maybe we should phone her and ask her if she'd like us to go over tonight."

Ann: Hmm.

Beth: Don't you want to?

Ann: Well . . . Well, yes . . . Well, maybe . . .

Beth: You sound hesitant.

Ann: Me?

Beth: Would you rather not go tonight?

Ann: No. Yes. No . . . I just feel awful. I feel as if I want to run away from the whole thing. But how could I do that to Emily?

Beth: Me too. It's so frightening to hear about this.

Ann: Yes, that's right. It brings it home. It feels so close. This makes it feel as if it can happen to me.

Beth: Maybe that's what we're talking about. I was just thinking the same thing. If we're feeling this scared, what must Emily be feeling?

Ann: Now I see.

Beth: What?

Ann: I think I was feeling it was selfish to be worrying about myself — how could I be scared when I should be thinking about Emily when she's facing this?

Beth: But we both just said how scared we were. Maybe that's just how it happens to anyone.

Ann: Well, it doesn't sound selfish to me when *you* say you're scared. Maybe it's okay . . . maybe that's really okay. But how terrible for Emily. How scared *she* must be . . . I really want to call her and go see her tonight. I'll feel better if I'm with her. I can just tell how awful it must be for her to be alone with these feelings.

Beth: She shouldn't be alone with this.

Ann and Beth continue to talk about what else they might do — accompany Emily to doctors, suggest she get a second opinion. Both still feel sad and fearful, but they feel connected by these feelings and able to take action.

But suppose Ann talks about Emily with a different friend or a family member or with her husband, Tom. After her first statement, made with tears in her eyes and a sad and fearful voice, Tom says, "Well, it's a terrible thing. In the end, she'll have to do the best she can. She should get a second opinion. I hear the Sloan Clinic is very good on these kinds of cases. Have you called her back yet?"

Tom pauses, apparently having settled that question. "Did you call my sister about the birthday party for my mother? We should really do something about that if it's going to come off."

Ann continues the conversation about the party and her role in arranging it because that is the focus of Tom's emotional interest. Like many women, Ann readily slips into going along on the other person's track — especially when the other person is a man. This accommodation often occurs without either person recognizing it. Because she is trying to stay in connection with Tom, Ann begins to lose touch with the texture of her own feelings. All she knows is that she now feels worse than she did before, and she dreads phoning Emily.

We won't pursue this interaction now except to note what may seem obvious — that it is not a growth-promoting one.

Instead, we'll focus in detail on the first conversation, between Ann and Beth, as an illustration of two aspects of connection that our colleague Janet Surrey has proposed are the basic processes of growth — mutual empathy and mutual empowerment.[1] (Throughout this book we will use the word *connection* to mean an interaction between two or more people that is mutually empathic and mutually empowering. We'll use *disconnection* to mean an encounter that works against mutual empathy and mutual empowerment. We'll use the word *relationship* to mean the set of interactions that occur over a length of time. A relationship may be composed of connections and disconnections, usually a mixture of both. We will be elaborating on these meanings as we go along.)

MUTUAL EMPATHY

The example of Ann and Beth may sound ordinary; people have conversations like this all the time. But the interchange between them is far from ordinary in terms of its value. Although the valuable actions Ann and Beth perform are often taken for granted, in fact, they contain the key features that make for psychological development in both children and adults.

Ann, as she starts this particular interchange, is experiencing several thoughts and feelings at the same time. (It is significant that there does not seem to be a common word in our language to convey the concept of "feeling-thoughts" or "thought-feelings" — that is, thoughts together with their accompanying emotions. This lack suggests the deep separation of thinking and feeling in our cultural concepts.)[2]

When Ann brings up the subject of Emily's illness, she conveys her sadness in words and in her emotional expression, that is, her tone of voice, the tears in her eyes, and her posture. She also conveys fear in her facial expression and her voice, although she has not yet put this fear into words.

At this point, Ann is not certain herself what her feelings are. Emotions usually come in mixtures; we rarely feel one clear, pure feeling, and we are rarely certain about what our feelings are until we have the chance to engage with another person who can resonate with them.

Beth responds with empathy, the capacity to feel and think something similar to the feelings and thoughts of another person that exists in all people; she puts the sadness they both feel into words and also expresses some fear in her face and voice.

What is especially growth-promoting is that as they talk, Beth shares both her own feelings and thoughts about Emily *and* those that arise in response to Ann's. (For example, she talks about the fear that *she* feels.) Because she does *both* of these things, she adds something to what Ann has expressed, and the two of them can move on to a fuller recognition of their thoughts and feelings, one that may not have been possible a moment before. This is emotional and cognitive (feeling-thinking) movement — it is action.

This extraordinarily important form of action is not usually recognized as such. As always, we have all incorporated male notions for the definition of the word. However, by responding to Ann's thoughts and feelings and by bringing forward those of her own, Beth is being very active. This is not a passive "just talking." It is the process that leads to forward movement — growth — and to taking further action in the world.

Not only does Beth respond to Ann, but Ann is able to receive Beth's response somewhat accurately, that is, to recognize that Beth is both feeling with her and adding something more. This is important, because it could happen differently: Ann might have replied, "No, I don't feel sad. We don't even know what's happening yet. Stop overreacting." Other manifestations of an inability to receive an empathic response can be more subtle, such as changing the subject right at this point, but in this conversation, Beth's response and Ann's reception of it make forward movement possible.

Next, Beth takes a step toward doing something, toward trying to be helpful, in her suggestion about visiting Emily. Now Ann hesitates. She's able to stay with her feelings enough to know that something isn't quite right, even if she can't yet clearly articulate what it is, and since she has felt Beth's empathy both now and in the past, she feels safe enough to be able to hesitate rather than hasten to agree with her or feel forced to do a "good deed" for Emily.

Responding to Ann's hesitation, Beth doesn't tell her what to do, nor is she critical. Instead, she respects Ann's hesitancy even though she doesn't fully understand it; she can tell she is not fully in tune with Ann, so she asks some questions.

The empathic tone of this exchange allows Ann to try to get to her feelings and express them more fully. Still unclear, she can simply say, "I just feel awful," and she can also go on to reveal, "I feel as if I want to run away from the whole thing." That is, Beth's response has given Ann the possibility of "trying again" or "trying some more," even though Beth's words have not yet fully spoken to everything she is experiencing.

Ann's honesty in grappling with her reaction to Emily's illness makes it possible for Beth to know her own fear: "Me too. It's so frightening . . ."

As Beth more fully understands herself through empathy with Ann's struggle to understand, she can receive Ann's fuller response to her, and Ann in turn can explore her own feelings and thoughts as they evolve in the interplay.

After both Ann and Beth express their fears more clearly, Beth feels a much greater direct link to Emily, the third friend, *through* these very fears: "If we're feeling this scared, what must Emily be feeling?" This statement makes it possible for Ann to see another part of her own mixture of emotions — her concern that she didn't have the right to feel afraid, that it would mean she was selfish. When Beth counters by recognizing that they both are experiencing similar feelings, Ann can take a different perspective on the question: because Beth doesn't seem selfish to her, she can begin to feel, in some measure, that her own fear for herself might be "okay."

Indeed, Ann's knowing her own fear puts her in better touch with the fear that Emily is probably feeling. Now Ann is impelled to be with Emily much more out of a growing sense of empathy with her and less out of a forced sense of obligation.

We've cut up this interplay rather mechanistically in order to discuss it, but the exchange itself is by no means mechanical. The essence of what has happened is movement and mutuality — emotional and cognitive action that benefits both people. Beth isn't simply sitting around being empathic to Ann. A larger relational dynamic is in progress, one in which both parties are being empathic. For example, Ann receives Beth's responses accurately because she herself is in tune with Beth, able to pick up, to know, Beth's feelings and thoughts, which are offered in response to her own. Ann and Beth are engaged *together* in the thoughts and feelings in this situation. This is what we mean by "mutual empathy."[3]

Mutual empathy is the great unsung human gift. We are all born with the possibility of engaging in it. Out of it flows mutual empowerment. It is something very different from one-way empathy; it is a joining together based on the authentic thoughts and feelings of all the participants in a relationship.

In our example, the dynamic of mutual empathy makes it possible for both Ann and Beth to keep adding something more to their dialogue. The "something more" creates the flow and change, the progression. Because each person can receive and then respond to the feelings and thoughts of the other, each is able to enlarge both her own feelings and thoughts *and* the feelings and thoughts of the other person. Simultaneously, each person enlarges the relationship.

MUTUAL EMPOWERMENT

We've said that mutual empathy leads to mutual empowerment. The best way to define mutual empowerment is to say it is composed of at least five components: "zest," action, knowledge, worth, and a desire for more connection.

"Zest" in Emotional Connection

In an interplay like the one we've described between Ann and Beth, each person experiences a greater sense of "zest," the feeling that comes when we feel a real sense of connection, of being together with and joined by another person. It feels like an increase — as opposed to a decrease — in vitality, aliveness, energy.

This feeling is there when people make emotional connections and it is notably absent when they do not. We can all probably remember its opposite, the "down" kind of feeling that we experience when we are not making an authentic connection with another person.

In our example, Ann feels more vitality or energy because Beth is *there*, with her in the course of exploring these feelings. To say that Ann feels an increase in energy does not mean that she necessarily feels less sad or even less fearful; it is to say that what matters is to be *in connection* with others, and with the feelings, whatever they are, that arise out of an experience.

As part of this basic emotional connection, Ann grows in several ways. First, she is able to state her feelings and thoughts directly, as they come to her as the interplay goes along — to represent her experience as it arises for her. This is movement toward greater authenticity. In addition, she gains in what could be called courage, the ability to put forward her feelings and thoughts to another person and to stand by them.

As Beth and Ann proceed in this connection, something else happens. Beth conveys that she cares for and is concerned about Ann, not in some static or abstract sense, but as "Ann-feeling-these-feelings-and-thinking-these-thoughts" in this moment. From many, many such experiences of connection, one can build the vitality that sustains psychological development. And it is from the (all too common) lack of these experiences that the reverse occurs.

Beth does not state her caring and concern by saying it in words explicitly; she conveys it by *going with* Ann in Ann's immediate experience. This is a part of what leads to the increase in zest, the energizing effect of the emotional joining.

We're struck, as we try to describe these elements in the flow of authentic emotional connection between people, by how often it seems easier to describe their opposites. We think this says something about how deeply our culture has failed to recognize or value such growth-fostering processes, and that it is significant that these are the parts of the human potential that have been assigned to women by patriarchal society.

The feeling of increased vitality and energy that comes from the sense of connection is the most basic feature of growth-fostering interactions — and leads directly to the next.

Action

First of all, Ann (and Beth, too) feels empowered to act *in the moment of the immediate exchange.* In this interplay each acts and has an important impact on the other — each creates change. This extremely valuable form of action in the immediate relational interplay is often overlooked, but it is a key form of action in its consequences for psychological development because it is only by interacting that we each affect each other. It is the way we play a part in augmenting or diminishing other people — and the relationships between people.

Next, as a result of the action within the immediate interplay — the conversation itself — Ann feels empowered to act in realms beyond, to be with Emily in a fuller way and to take action within her relationship with Emily. Prior to her exchange with Beth, Ann had felt hesitation and conflict about facing this difficult situation. But as her interactions with Beth proceed, she becomes more able and more motivated to help Emily get a second opinion, or to go with her for doctors' visits.

Knowledge

As a result of their conversation, Ann and Beth have each made a step toward an enlarged and more accurate picture of themselves and of each other. Ann knows more about her sadness and about Beth's sadness as she experiences these with Beth, and she has learned a bit more about her own and Beth's fears. They both also know a little more about their relationship and how it can encompass these experiences. This is how we gradually come to know ourselves and others — and learn about how the world goes.

Moreover, Ann can now see more clearly why and how she feels fearful, and she can have the fear without linking it with selfishness. With this distinction now more evident, Ann becomes aware of the extent of her true sadness and concern for Emily — her feeling *with* Emily. Before this exchange with Beth, her concern, her sadness, and her fear were obscured in the emotional knot that included "selfishness" — and this confusion was detracting from her sense of worth.

Sense of Worth

Ann feels a bit more worthwhile as a person *because* she has felt worthwhile in her interchange with Beth, worthwhile as "Ann-thinking-these-thoughts-and-feeling-these-feelings." Beth's responsiveness conveyed to Ann a picture of herself as someone worthy of another person's recognition and attention in the experiencing of these feelings and thoughts.

We cannot develop a sense of worth unless the people important to us convey that they recognize and acknowledge our experience. Adults often do this for infants and children, of course. If a child expresses distress, adults try to figure out what the matter is, and to respond. Is the child afraid or tired or hungry? Or, if a child is joyous, or just "hanging out," they join the child in that mode or mood, and the child feels attended to and recognized. This attention and recognition are just as vital for adults and must be present all through life — or else we suffer terribly.

Beth does not reinforce the negative characterization of Ann as selfish — quite the reverse — and this adds significantly to Ann's feeling more worthy. It is really a great benefit to Ann to know that her feeling of fear is a common and appropriate response to such a situation.

By contrast, we are diminished when feelings arise in us that we have been taught to label bad or unacceptable. For women, one of the common negative labels is "selfish." For many women, this word has been linked with so many feelings that it can come to seem that almost any feeling is a selfish one. For men, the negative labels are usually different. It is rare to hear men worry about being selfish for feeling a certain way, but it is common for men to worry about feeling weak or "soft."

While making the distinction between fear and selfishness is important in itself, it also helps Ann augment her sense of worthiness in another way. She can now move toward Emily, and toward action with Emily, and taking these steps further enhances her picture of herself. She is now doing something to allay her own fear (not just for Emily), and this active engagement with her emotions makes her feel even more worthwhile. Feeling unable to act, to do something constructive in the face of her fear, would have made her feel less worthy. (Indeed, at times people fall into doing something that does not attend to the crucial feeling involved — for example, eating, drinking, sleeping, or overworking — to escape it.)

Finally, when someone else "goes with us in the feelings" we are more able to believe that our feelings are legitimate. In this example, Beth stepped right "in there," grappling with her own fears and becoming more connected to Ann as their interplay proceeded. To feel more connected with others in the course of experiencing one's feelings — rather than less connected — also builds a sense of worth.

Greater Sense of Connection and
Desire for More Connections

As a result of the increased "zest," empowerment, knowledge, and worth in connection, Ann now also feels more concern and caring for Beth. This feeling is different from being the recipient of another's concern, or being loved, and very different from feeling "approved of." It is much more valuable. It is the active, outgoing feeling of caring about another person because that person means so much to us or is so valued in our eyes. It leads to both the desire for fuller connection with that person and a concern for that person's well-being. We cannot will this feeling into existence. It comes along as a concomitant of connection. And it leads to wanting more connection with others as well.

Ann feels the motivation and energy to reach beyond her relationship with Beth, toward a connection with Emily. Ann's "fear about her fear" and her conflict around the issue of selfishness could have stood in the way of her access to the other feelings she has about Emily. But her feelings of caring and concern have now moved into more clarity and prominence. To the extent that the confusion about fear and selfishness persisted, they would have prevented Ann from connecting with Emily in a fruitful way (at this time Emily doesn't really need Ann's self-blame and the like).

Ann feels zestful and enlarged and is moved to continue this process with other people. Indeed, one way of thinking about the essentials for growth-fostering interactions is to ask: Does this interaction lead to a greater sense of connection with the person(s) directly involved — *and* does it lead to the motivation for more connection in general? Or does it lead to the reverse, to a turn toward isolation?

MUTUALITY AND GROWTH

We can now talk about some of the characteristics of this interplay as they lead to Beth's psychological growth. Here again, their interchange is mutual.

At first, Beth responds to Ann because people, at bottom, simply do respond to each other's feelings unless something else interferes. Beth's response gives her a sense of connection with another person that is gratifying and energy producing in itself, just as it is for Ann. This point is often overlooked. People experience pleasure if they can respond to another person's feelings with feelings of their own, regardless of what the feelings themselves are. We experience pleasure in this, *per se* — the feeling of being in the flow of human connection rather than out of it. (The latter is a terrible feeling, one we have all experienced.) Connection in this sense does not depend upon whether the feelings are happy or sad or something else; it means having feelings *with* another person, aside from the specific nature of the feelings.

The phenomenon of empathy is basic to all our relationships. Either we deal with the feelings that are inevitably present in our interactions by turning to each other — or we turn away. If we turn away from others without conveying a recognition of the existence of their feelings, we inevitably leave the other person diminished in some degree. We also are inevitably turning away from engaging fully with our own experience, dealing with it in a less than optimal way — that is, in isolation.

Of course, there are times when any one person may not be empathic to another, especially in situations where society specifically discourages people from using this ability. (People trained to be warriors would not be encouraged to develop empathy.) Also, there are times when we may pick up the feelings of another person, but disagree with the perceptions that are leading to these feelings. For example, suppose Beth thought that Emily was a hypochondriac and that her situation probably wasn't serious. Beth might pick up Ann's feelings but not share them. Their interaction might still lead to empathy, but through a more complex route.

For the moment, the point is that Beth was also dealing with her *own* feelings as soon as the interplay got under way — not just Ann's. Because she could enter into empathy with Ann, Beth came to know a bit more about her own sadness and her own fears.

Beth, like Ann, was empowered to act within the relationship and she too felt this action as a source of worth. Further, people tend to feel empowered and worthy if they feel they have an effect — an impact — on others. It is a pleasurable feeling.

In contrast is the feeling that we cannot have an impact, that no matter how we try, we can't seem to reach the other person. A common minor example is having someone leave the room when you're trying to say something to her/him. Even more common, but more subtle and sometimes more confusing, is the experience of feeling that someone is "turning off," psychologically leaving the scene.

In the course of life, each person builds a basic inner sense of his or her ability to act — of empowerment — as a result of the experience of seeing that he or she can have an impact on others. This means, of course, that we also acquire more ability to act because of other people's responses to us — their impact on us. That is, action emerges out of the interplay, not out of one person as a sole, individual actor. We all develop our abilities to act as a result of our interactions throughout life. (Infants are born with a repertoire of abilities and the potential for the growth of many more.)

Out of the experience of authentic, mutually empathic interactions, we acquire the "feeling-thinking" understanding of ourselves and others that gives us a sense of a "knowledgeable" basis for action. Most of us, we believe, would develop more capacities for action, and ways to be active, if we had optimal mutual relationships.

SOURCES OF ACTION

The kind of action we have seen in the interplay between Ann and Beth is very different from the way we usually depict action in our culture. As our colleagues Judith Jordan and Janet Surrey have explained, our society tends to portray and value action as the result of the forceful exertion of the lone individual.[4] That is, each person should make up his or her own mind. Take decisive steps. Demonstrate ability, strength, power. (Tom was reflecting this approach in his advice for Ann to give to Beth: "Do the best you can. Get a second opinion. Go to the Sloan Clinic.") But here we argue that action takes a variety of forms, with great cultural and individual variation in the preferences and patterns. There are differences present even in newborn babies; each baby is active in her/his own way.

An important distortion of the concept of action arises from our patriarchal culture, especially in the United States. Men in particular are pressured to be individual actors, not to seek a basis for action *in their relationships.* This often leads to a leap to find a way to take action as a *substitute* for experiencing the feelings at hand and to a pressure to act even if a sound basis for action doesn't exist or if one feels uncertain.

Men in particular often take action even when in order to do so they must override feelings such as doubt, confusion, and uncertainty. (Some rush into action even more swiftly if they feel uncertain.) Action is valued in itself and men are taught to condemn themselves and others for anything that looks "passive." Because of this pressure, they often force themselves, and others, to act in ways that ignore even their own more complicated and multifaceted feelings.

The example of Ann and Tom, in which Ann defers to Tom's lead, illustrates this point and contrasts with Ann and Beth's interplay. In the conversation with his wife, Tom immediately advises action about Emily and then quickly moves on to more advice on action about the party. Beth, unlike Tom, trusts Ann's initial hesitation, and together she and Ann move into this feeling and explore its connections to other feelings and thoughts. As a result, they both arrive at a basis for action that emerges out of a greater clarity and strength of thinking and feeling.

In general, in our culture women have been encouraged to provide support for men's actions. While many men have received a great deal of empathy that has helped them become empowered, often they have not been aware of it. Because women have been attuned to the fact that men have difficulty acknowledging such needs, they often provided for them subtly and sensitively. At the same time, most women have not received from men the same empathic attention to their experience nor the support for their actions that would flow from mutually empathic interactions. And this imbalance has not provided either women or men with the kind of optimal mutual empathy that leads to mutual empowerment.

MUTUAL RATHER THAN
INDIVIDUAL DEVELOPMENT

We want to stress that we are not talking about "communication" alone, important as that is. We are trying to demonstrate how people develop within connections.

We have talked about Ann and Beth's interchange in detail in order to try to illustrate how each individual's growth occurs as a result of her interaction with another person. But the more important point is that through their interaction they have created something new together. *Both* are enlarged by this creation. Something new now exists, built by both of them. This is what we call "the connection between." It does not belong to one or the other; it belongs to both. Yet each feels it as "hers," as part of her. She contributed to its creation, and it contributed to her, to what she now "is," which is more than she was a few moments before.

This is one way of beginning to talk about what a growth-fostering relationship is. The elements of connection can be seen as trends and flows that go on over time in many thousands of interchanges. However, at each moment, we do or say things that tend to open up the possibilities for growth-fostering processes to occur or tend to close them down.

While our vignette about Ann and Beth does not tell the total story of a true relationship, the basic processes it illustrates are real. A great many people are participating in these growth-fostering processes all the time. If no one did, no person would survive or grow at all. Although women themselves often have a great deal of trouble recognizing the growth-fostering interchanges in which they engage, millions of women have responded and interacted in these ways for centuries. Yet in psychology, these processes have been couched in global and mystifying terms — "the maternal instinct," "symbiotic states with infants," "nurturing," even "being a good wife" — labels that distance the process and render it a side issue.

Of course, all women aren't mutually empathic and empowering all the time, nor are all men the reverse. However, differences in the ways men and women tend to interact do exist at this time in history, and we believe they are the result of the different kinds of behavior that have been encouraged for women and men. Certainly, some men know a great deal about empathy and mutuality. In general, however, men have been encouraged to turn away from learning about this aspect of experience because this part of life has been said to be womanly.

Even under optimal conditions, relationships would be composed of both connections and disconnections. In fact, relationships have to encompass many disparate and conflicting thoughts and feelings. There has to be room to deal with oppositional or negative and destructive thoughts and feelings as well as misperceptions and misunderstandings. In Ann's encounter with Tom, she has an additional and more arduous task. If she is to deal with what she feels is wrong or lacking in his response as she experiences it, she will have to work at changing the direction of the interaction. But people can do this. In general, so long as one person can see a possibility of engaging with another in thoughts and feelings — the possibility of connecting — she or he can work toward realizing it.

Of course, the other person has to be able to engage with the matter at hand, to enter into the movement of thoughts and feelings. If one person has more power in a relationship, it is more difficult for the less powerful person to bring about such an engagement. And it is when there seems to be no possibility of engaging with the feelings and thoughts at hand, no way to move within the relationship, that the most trouble occurs. (The problem of interchanges that are not growth-promoting, or are even destructive, is a large one, which we will explore more thoroughly in subsequent chapters.)

The more growth-promoting interactions we have had, the better our base of psychological resources will be, to help us deal with difficult and conflictual interactions. Conflictual interactions can lead to growth too — so long as there is a possibility of really engaging.

RELATIONAL IMAGES

As psychological growth occurs in our interplay with others, we believe, our notions of who we are — and who other people are — are formed. Thus people create in their minds relational images, images that portray the patterns of their relational experience. These images also embody what each person expects will happen in future relationships as they unfold.

If we all had experiences like Ann and Beth's all the time, we would form images of relationships that are mutually empathic and give us the means and motivation to act — connections that lead us to more knowledge, that make us feel worthwhile and eager for more connections, that help problematic situations resolve into solutions.

People also create explanations about *why* their relationships are the way they are. Thus, out of a connection like Ann and Beth's, we would construct the explanation or meaning that we are each valuable, worthwhile, knowledgeable, active people. These constructions, we believe, determine our beliefs about ourselves and others in all areas of our lives.

In fact, all of our experiences are not like Ann and Beth's. Many are like Ann and Tom's; many are much worse. From such experiences — which we call *dis*connections — we create very different relational images. For example, from the interchange with Tom, Ann might form an image of relationships in which feelings cannot be heard, understood, or engaged with mutually; in which she is unable to act or to change a situation; in which she feels less worthwhile and which demonstrate that trying to connect with an important person in her life leaves her feeling more isolated and more alone.

From many such experiences she could derive the meaning that she is an ineffective person. Moreover, she might come to believe that she is an undesirable person, since the important person in her life doesn't seem to care about or value her experience. (Indeed, the consequences can be much worse. We will elaborate more on how disconnections lead to restricted relational images and disparaging meanings in Chapter 4.)

It is clear that most of us possess a complicated mélange of relational images and meanings. We begin creating them early in life and then elaborate on them and revise them throughout life. Much of this process goes on outside of awareness. If we have built images that allow us some opening to take in new relational experiences, our images and meanings can keep growing, and this in turn can encourage us to change further and to explore new experiences in our relationships. However, if we have experienced many disconnections, our relational images will lead us away from engagement with other people. If this is the case, our relational images will not grow and change; they can become quite fixed.[5]

Even when we are alone, we are thinking, feeling, and acting within a framework formed by these images and their meanings. If they have been growth-fostering, we have a rich and multifaceted framework in which to function. At the same time, we need ongoing connections to keep this framework alive and growing. Few of us can live in isolation from other people, though there are many cultural and individual variations in the amount and style of interplay that suits each person best.

If we have had many interactions that have allowed us to express our experience at each stage in life as fully as possible, and if we have been able to respond to and have an impact on others, we will carry within us the courage and the desire to keep trying to express our experience within connections to others. It is usually the parts of our experience that we feel we cannot share that make trouble for us, the parts we have walled off because we've been led to believe that we cannot bring them into a relational connection. Before we discuss these matters, it is important to consider some of the wider implications of mutual empathy, mutual empowerment, and growth-fostering connections.

3

A PARADIGM SHIFT

Ann and Beth lead us to central issues in psychology and society. We have said that mutual empathy and mutual empowerment in relationships are central to psychological growth. These concepts are so fundamental and yet so foreign to prevalent descriptions of psychological development that it is important to examine them further and to see where they take us.

We are at the very beginning of trying to understand growth-fostering relationships and to describe their necessary transformation to *mutually* growth-fostering relationships, but Judith Jordan's work on empathy and mutuality provides a basic framework.[1] Earlier, Heinz Kohut and other self psychologists directed major attention to empathy.[2] Jordan has added important emphases to the concept. She stresses that empathy is an *ability*, requiring a complex integration of cognitive and emotional (thinking and feeling) capacities, rather than a mysterious, intuitive, or even regressive state, as some have suggested. (Interestingly, all of the latter terms were often given negative connotations when empathy was linked to women.)

Our ability to be empathic provides the basic foundation of human connection. To the idea of empathy, Jordan and Janet Surrey have added the crucial concept of mutuality. Just as we can get a sense of how another person feels and thinks, so others can get a sense of how we feel and think, and as this mutual empathy flows we create something much more than "one-way" empathy. We create a joining together in a shared experience that builds something new for both (or all) of the people involved as Ann and Beth did.[3]

As we are using the word, mutuality does not mean sameness, nor does it mean equality; rather it means a way of relating, a shared activity in which each (or all) of the people involved are participating as fully as possible.

Surrey states that "mutuality describes a creative process, in which openness to change allows something new to happen, building on the different contributions of each person" — as we saw with Ann and Beth. In seeking to clarify this concept further, she explains, "Mutual empathy is not so much a matter of reciprocity — 'I give to you and then you give to me' — an 'equal-time doctrine' — but rather a quality of relationality, a movement or dynamic of relationship. . . . The capacity to participate in mutually empathic relationships can replace the concept of the *need for* or *need to provide* empathy."[4]

For example, Helen and her two-year-old, Kathy, are building with large blocks. They take turns placing one block on top of another. Each time the blocks reach a certain height the whole pile topples over. Kathy laughs with great glee and Helen responds with great laughter evoked by Kathy's laughter. Each has a different level of skill and each contributes differently, but each can participate fully in the activity.

The most important part of the activity is not the specifics of what each does but how they relate to each other. While Helen is not primarily interested in Kathy's "achievement" as a builder, she's

delighted with her child's interest and activity. She is thrilled by Kathy's lively participation and Kathy is thrilled by the sight and sound
of blocks falling *and* by her mother's joining with her in this en-
joyment.

Although Helen does not think about it explicitly, she grows a
little step in feeling she's a good mother; she's participated in bringing about the child's happiness and growth. The child grows in her
motor abilities and, more importantly, in her sense of herself as
someone who can engage with this important other person, her
mother, and who feels her mother wanting to engage with her. Hel-
en's participation in her child's pleasure conveys to Kathy that she
has had an impact on her mother; she's participated in bringing
about her mother's happiness.

This vignette offers a vivid illustration of mutual empathy — an
example where power differentials don't preclude genuine mutuality. Thus a parent and child, teacher and student, or therapist and patient can and do engage in mutual empathy. Each may contribute at
a different level of empathy based on her/his age and experience,
but each can be fully engaged in their shared activity and this action
advances each person's psychological development.

RESONANCE AND RESPONSE

From infancy on, children and adults want — and need — to be engaged with others. Even very young children respond to the feelings
of others and want (and need) to "understand" these feelings as
completely as they can. Suppose Helen suddenly changed from her
usual interest and joy in the block building, Kathy would feel this
and would want to know what was going on, although she may not
yet be able to put her question into words. (Of course, Kathy experiences this at a two-year-old, not an adult, level.) Helen's feelings
are an integral part of Kathy's world and affect her deeply; they influence her whole sense of who she is and what the world is like.

We have discussed how Ann and Beth as adults need mutual empathy. It is even more important for children. Children need to learn
about their own thoughts and feelings, and in order to do that they

need others who can be mutually empathic with them, can resonate with them and respond to them — can join with them in these thoughts and feelings. Indeed, we believe that all people need this resonance and response in order to even *experience* their important feelings in all of their depth and complexity.

Another way to put this central point is to say that when we talk about being in connection we mean being emotionally accessible, and to learn how to be emotionally accessible we need the experience of being in connection. Without this interplay with others, we cannot know and understand our own thoughts and feelings. We need other people who can engage with us about the important parts of our experience, not at every moment but as an ongoing part of our lives.

Further, we need other people who can join with us in both our "good" and our "bad" feelings and we suffer if people do not join us, at least sometimes, in the full range of feelings that inevitably arise as we go through life. For example, Lucy, a four-year-old child who pursued her curiosities and interests with glee, was told to "quiet down" by parents who could not tolerate her exuberance. (Another child might get the same message more subtly, but still powerfully, just because her parents do not join her in her joy.) She does not like the isolation she feels when she is joyous. Is there something wrong with feeling gleeful? What does that mean? Is something wrong with her? In time, Lucy's glee may become confused with these other feelings and she will lose her knowledge of the experience of joy. She will no longer know clearly what her experience is.

In similar fashion, many parents who cannot themselves find a way to bring their experience into relationships may in a sense "forbid" their children the experience of distress or sadness. (This is especially likely to happen if the parents have caused the distress, but it can occur even if they did not.) As a result, the child cannot feel able to express and know these feelings for what they are. A very common example is telling a child not to cry. In one family, a newborn baby died. The parents kept telling their one other child, Margaret, a four-year-old, to "be a big girl" and not to cry. While this particular admonition is more likely to happen to boys because of cultural dictates, it happens to girls, too, especially when the child's distress or sadness touches the parents in their own sadness.

A forty-year-old woman whose parents were both Holocaust survivors told of a silent but even more powerful control. She recalled that, in her adolescent years, when she would come home unhappy or troubled her mother would look at her face and then abruptly turn away. She felt erased at those moments, ashamed of her unhappiness, and very alone. She came to believe that her sad feelings were somehow bad, that she was a bad person to have these feelings, and that she ought not to have them because such feelings would hurt and distress her mother.

In contrast, as we have seen in the Ann and Beth story, out of mutual empathy comes mutual empowerment. All people, whether infants, children, or adults, are energized for action following mutually empathic encounters. Helen and Kathy, who were building with blocks, were each empowered to carry on several activities — Kathy to develop more eye-hand coordination, fine-muscle movement, and the like, and, more importantly, to engage with her mother; and Helen to become enlarged in her abilities to participate in a growth-enhancing connection. In an example on a larger scale, out of mutual empathy many women from battered women's shelters become empowered to join with others to undertake legal and political action to try to prevent wife-battering.

In our experience as psychotherapists and in other work over many years, we find that when a person feels that another is empathic, she can often move into action instead of feeling ineffective or immobilized. In fact, as we shall explain, a therapist's engagement in mutual empathy with the patient is the key factor leading not just to understanding, but to active change. We have often seen that as a therapist truly engages with a woman who is depressed and stuck, for instance, and she believes her therapist is truly with her, she can move toward action. That action may be a small step at first, but it can take enormous courage — for example, trying a phone call to a friend after being withdrawn from everyone — and it can be the start out of a depressive spiral.

Mutual empowerment is very different from a power-over way of operating. As a basic shift in thinking, we can unlink the concept of power from the concept of domination. The power of people to interact so that *both* benefit is unlimited. It is possible to create repeatedly more of this kind of power. Through mutually empowering interactions people can find the "power to do," to act effectively in the world.

Seen in this framework, the goal of development means the increasing ability to build and enlarge mutually enhancing relationships in which each person can feel an increased sense of well-being through being in touch with others and finding ways to act on her or his thoughts and feelings.[5]

Each individual can develop a larger and more complex repertoire and can contribute to, and grow from, more complex relationships. The goal is not an increasing sense of separation, but one of enhanced connection — and this connection in turn leads to more enlargement and enhancement of each person, and so on in a growing cycle.

Each person may grow at a different rate. Helen and Kathy building with blocks offer a vivid illustration of this point. A parent and child, teacher and student, or therapist and patient can and do engage in mutual empathy and mutual empowerment. Each may contribute a different kind of action based on her/his age, role, or experience, but each can be fully engaged in, and affected by, their shared activity.

PARTICIPATION
RATHER THAN GRATIFICATION

Our colleague Alexandra Kaplan has suggested that *the* basic human motive, if we can speak of such a thing, can be better understood as the motive to *participate in connection with others*, rather than the need to be gratified by others.[6] The latter has long been a premise basic to psychodynamic theories and assumed in popular writing, though not usually explicitly. That is, most formulations begin with an *individual* whose basic motivation is to fulfill his drives: he should get what he wants. (Clearly this individual was a "he.") This assumption reflects the worldview of Western European and North American cultures.

Freud made clear his view on the centrality of gratification with his emphasis on drives that had to be satisfied. Even the many relational theorists who have departed from Freudian theory in other realms have retained the assumption that the drive toward gratification is the basic human motive. In the Freudian framework, the infant or child requires a kind of optimal gratification at each stage in life. If the child receives too little or too much s/he becomes fixated, stuck at that stage, and this fixation is the cause of psychological problems. For example, in Freudian thinking, in the oral stage, the first stage of life, the infant's drives are said to be centered around the mouth, as in sucking and eating. If her/his mother does not satisfy the drive adequately, the child will grow into a person who is constantly seeking to satisfy this drive by being dependent on another person. The person supplying the gratification, the "object" of the drive, is usually the woman, the mother.

As Kaplan notes, even W. D. R. Fairbairn, the founder of object relations theory (a relational theory), stated that the human being is basically "object seeking,"[7] by which he meant that the human being seeks to obtain gratification from the "object" (the use of the word "object" to mean "person" comes from Freud's original language about the "object" of the drive). A change of perspective on what constitutes the basic human motive, from being gratified to participating, represents our central shift from traditional approaches — it's not a question of *getting* but of *engaging* with others.

It is not, of course, that we are opposed to people being gratified; what we are questioning is a certain model as the basis of a theory of *psychological* development. Indeed, modern infant research does not view the infant or child as a passive being waiting to be gratified but as an active being participating in relationships, and researchers have demonstrated this active participation by even very young infants. Daniel Stern, Edward Tronick, Beatrice Beebe, and others have demonstrated the ways in which infants are exquisitely equipped to relate to other people and do so from earliest life. For example, within the first twenty-four hours of life, infants can distinguish their mothers' voices from other voices. The issue is the evolution of enlarging forms of relationship as the child matures, not the search for gratification — or separation from others.[8]

MUTUALITY VERSUS POWER-OVER

We know we live in a world that is not based on mutuality. Whenever one group of people has power over another, this creates disconnections and violations of the relationships between the members of the two groups. Indeed, by definition a dominant group is not likely to create mutually empowering relationships, else it would not remain dominant. Thus, a patriarchal society would not evolve a system of relationships based in mutuality. Instead, such a society tends to create a concept of power as a limited commodity and a "power-over" definition of power itself. This concept suffuses the dominant group's framework for all relationships throughout society, from the most large-scale to the most intimate.

The power-over model has been apparent in the way dominant groups treat people whom they define as different from them, that is, those labeled as belonging to other classes, races, ethnic groups, religions, or sexual preference. Although there are very specific ways in which each dominant group treats other groups, overall it has been, and is, considered acceptable to exploit or colonize whole groups of people. The effects of this destructive treatment are manifold and add to the complexities of relationships between men and women in each group.

Of course, women do not escape the influence of this power-over system; all of us have incorporated it to varying degrees, along with the racism, classism, and heterosexism that surrounds us. In recent years, women have been writing on the specifics of their experience in these complicated situations and of the effects of being doubly or triply oppressed by the intertwining effects of class, racism, sexism, and heterosexism.[9] All forms of oppression are also relational oppression; they act against mutual relationships and therefore create major disconnections between people who come from different groups. Further, as many recent writers have taught us, these groupings of people are not givens, or "natural groups"; they are socially constructed out of the thinking and practice of dominant groups.

We are proposing that cultures built on dominant-subordinate relationships based on gender as well as class, race, and other characteristics have created a nonmutual model that permeates all relationships. We *all* have developed within this framework and it tends to determine the nature of even our most intimate relationships. On the other hand, even within the dominant framework, some people in the United States experience more communality in their families and communities because of their cultural traditions — for example, African Americans, Native Americans, and Latinos/as — and almost all of us have had at least some glimpses of mutuality. As we've suggested, this is possible because for human beings to survive, someone has to provide growth-fostering relationships, and historically this activity has been assigned primarily to women.

From the growth-fostering relationships that we can glimpse at this time in our history, we can envision more fully mutual relationships for everyone. Meanwhile, however, we live in a society in which the dominant-subordinate framework affects us all and tends to lead to serious disconnections.

DISCONNECTIONS

We propose that psychological troubles follow from those situations in which one person or group has more power than another and can thereby create and enforce disconnections and violations. We will spell out the complex psychological effects produced by disconnections and trace the paths from serious disconnections to what comes to be called psychopathology. In doing so, we will see the link between social structure and the creation of psychological suffering.

This approach creates a focus on what we might call relational dynamics, including an exploration of how the "outside" becomes the "inside," that is, how our experience of either mutual or nonmutual relationships creates the internal psychic relational images that we discussed in Chapter 2. Our approach views the individual in the setting of her/his family and other immediate relational contexts, which, in turn, can be constituted only within an overall societal structure.

We will describe in detail the problematic relational images we each construct when we experience disconnections. As a brief example, recall two of the images that Lucy, the child whose parents could not join her in joy, constructed: that she will be alone if she feels joyous, and that something is wrong with her feeling joyous.

As we are using the word, disconnections occur whenever a relationship is not mutually empathic and mutually empowering (which means we experience disconnections often). The degree of disconnection can vary from a very minor feeling of being out of touch to major trauma and violation. For example, a seven-year-old girl, Marie, came home from school thrilled to tell her father that she was selected to be in the school play. Her father responded by asking her what she had gotten on her math exam. This is a disconnection. But it is not of the same magnitude as the disconnection and violation experienced by another seven-year-old, Nancy, who came home to a father who repeatedly raped her.

(We are not using the word "disconnection" to mean leaving a relationship, but rather to mean a break in connection accompanied by a sense of being cut off from the other person[s]. Sometimes leaving a relationship can be a wise thing to do if attempts to change a destructive situation reach insurmountable obstacles, but that is a different topic.)

In the chapters to follow we will be talking in detail about the instances in which an individual, like Nancy, cannot leave the relationship. This is the case in many institutions in which we have to live and work. Most important, it is always harder for the person or group with less power to change a relationship. This applies to adults, for example, in the workplace, and to children and some adults in families. It applies, too, to all groups of people who are marginalized, that is, deemed different and less valuable in our society on the basis of race, sexual preference, or other characteristics. All marginalized people have to find a way to deal with, and work to change, the nonmutual relationships that they cannot leave.

Up to now, in our culture, our central formative relationships have not been based in mutuality. Except for those few families that have made strenuous efforts to overcome their surrounding culture, we have all grown up being powerfully influenced by a patriarchal power-over model. Within this model, it is common to find that adults of both genders have not been able to act within relationships in ways that fully engage with the issues in their lives and allow them to flourish. To the extent that adults have not had those possibilities, we have difficulty providing an optimal relational context for children. For example, Margaret's parents, who lost a newborn baby, had both grown up in nonresponsive families, and this made them less likely to find ways together to know and respond to their child's concerns.

It seems fair to say that until recently, the overall message from society has been that men will do "the important things"; women will tend to the "lesser business" of trying to provide the growth-making relationships that are essential for everyone. To say this is not to say that women always succeed; it is to say that most women have tried. And they have done so in a context of "anti-mutuality": no one else was devoted to providing growth-fostering relationships; indeed, women were often denigrated for trying to do this, while living in a society that supported domination and even violence within the immediate family as well as in the surrounding society.

MOVEMENT IN RELATIONSHIP
RATHER THAN SEPARATION

As we suggested in Chapter 1, a focus on "the self" is central to almost all of modern psychodynamic thinking. We believe this reflects the individualistic bias of Western European and North American cultural concepts. The term has become so reified it's worth remembering that there is no such *thing* as a self. It is a *concept* made up by psychologists and sociologists.

We are concerned with people becoming increasingly authentic and that they become strong, active initiators and responders *within* connections. Toward that end, rather than focusing on static states of the individual, we have shifted our attention to the dynamics of relationships.

Ann and Beth illustrate this point. We think it is more important to understand how they made the flow — the growth — happen in their interchange than it is to ask, What kind of a self does each person have?

Thus we focus on the question of "movement in relationship." As Janet Surrey writes, "*Connection* has replaced *self* as the core element or the locus of the creative energy of development."[10] Can people grow within a given relationship? What will help to bring about such movement? What gets in the way?

By definition, relationships are moving, dynamic processes, not static entities. In our work we are continually struggling to find the ways to capture and describe this movement. Again, the language sounds strange — we have to use a long phrase like "movement in relationship" rather than one word — and (again) we believe this is because our culture has not honored certain experiences and so does not provide us with ready words to describe them.

In years of doing therapy, we have found that what matters in people's lives is whether they can feel that they are moving, that they can make something happen — not that everything be resolved but that they can see a way to act as opposed to feeling stuck in a condition of immobility and stagnation, with its usual accompaniments, hopelessness and despair.

Similarly, in thinking about development all through life, we believe that the central question is whether relationships can change so that they can allow and encourage expansion. For example, adolescents do not need "separation" from their parents, they need *change* in their relationships with their parents, the changes that their new abilities require; indeed, they need to preserve a deep underlying sense of connection with their parents. If they can feel this kind of truly trustworthy connection, they will be able to undertake the changes they need to make.[11]

Understanding this difference shifts our whole concept of growth from childhood through adolescence and adulthood. Our colleague Niki Fedele related a vivid example: A hospitalized late-adolescent woman who was in severe psychological distress had a father who was clearly very domineering and controlling. In line with standard practice, the hospital staff kept telling the father he had to "let his daughter separate from the family." The more the father heard this, the more controlling he became and the more defiant was his daughter. Finally, Niki, who has a relational approach, advised the staff to say to the father, "Your daughter needs you now more than ever. She needs you to help her find the ways to grow into a young woman." On hearing this, the father's anxiety diminished: he did not have to *leave* his daughter. He could be helped to refocus on trying to find the ways to help her to bring forward her perceptions and thoughts as they were in the present, not as they were in his image of her as a child.[12]

While this relationship did not have to be more distant, it did have to be different than it had been. It had to be more mutual, with room for more of the daughter's expression of herself as she was now and as she was struggling to become. The father could show his loving and supportive side but he *did* have to *change*; in turn, the daughter could drop some of her more recalcitrant behavior and begin to grow again.

In this movement and growth in relationship, the individual needs to represent her/his true experience — that is, she or he needs authenticity — *and also* to respond authentically to the thoughts and feelings of others. The latter has usually been omitted in talking about such concepts as the self, autonomy, and the like. Authenticity is not a static state that is achieved at a discrete moment in time; it is a person's ongoing ability to represent her-/himself in a relationship with increasing truth and fullness. Engagement in growth-enhancing relationships is precisely the process that leads to the possibility of speaking one's true thoughts and feelings. Ann and Beth illustrate this point. Here lies the empowerment that allows each person to risk such truthfulness and, in turn, leads each person on to more knowledge of her-/himself — the knowledge that emerges only out of true engagement with others.

If we don't have other people in our lives who can resonate and respond, we become less and less able to state our feelings and thoughts or even to know them. So it was that Lucy, the little girl who was so gleeful, came to lose her sense of her own experience.

Moreover she lost the sense that expressing her feelings was a good thing to do. If we have found it disconnecting and dangerous to put forward our feelings and thoughts, we begin to focus on methods of not representing our perceptions and feelings. We start down a path away from knowledge of ourselves and away from a sense of authenticity.

We consider autonomy in a similar way. That is, we would emphasize that the individual must be able to represent her/his experience, her/his thoughts and feelings, with increasing authenticity. S/he must be able to say "This is important to me" and also "It's important to me that you know this is important to me." Individuals need to be present *and* active *and* engaged with other individuals.

Coming out of a history of restriction, women and other marginalized people especially need a sense of freedom and authenticity, a sense of the right to pursue what is important to them and to use all of their capacities. Participating in connections does not mean sacrificing the individual to the group or to "the team," nor does it mean being altruistic. On the contrary, it means that each individual has both the responsibility to represent her-/himself as fully as possible *and* the responsibility to respond to others. If we do not respond there is no flow, no movement. If, in fact, psychological development occurs only in interaction with other people, do we not all have the responsibility to be responsive to others? Who else will do this for us if not each other?[13]

Nor does this kind of relationship seek to diminish each person's uniqueness; indeed, the uniqueness can strengthen rather than detract from the relationship. Helen and Kathy, the mother and baby, each made her unique contribution to that interplay. Neither one could possibly be like the other.

To emphasize psychological growth within connections does not mean that people have to be in interaction all the time. Also, people have their varying styles and rhythms. As Judith Jordan says,

Our perspective appreciates that . . . people experience a sense of personal history, continuity and coherence; that we demonstrate initiative and responsiveness; that we feel bodily sensations and limits; that we are aware of emotions and organize our ex-

perience in meaningful ways. We also view solitude, feeling effective in our work, and relating to the whole non-human environment as essential human experiences. But our perspective
stresses that we thrive in being in connection. We acknowledge
intrapsychic reality,[14] but we see context, the ongoing relational
interplay between self and other, as primary to real growth and
vitality. We are suggesting a shift from a psychology of "entities"
to a psychology of movement and dialogue. The goal of development is not the creation of a bounded entity with independent internal psychic structure that turns to the outside world
only in a state of need or deficiency. On the contrary, in the ideal
pattern of development, we move toward participation in relational growth rather than toward simple attainment of personal
gratification. . . . In fact, self, other, and the relationship are no
longer clearly separated entities in this perspective but are seen
as *mutually forming processes.*[15]

Ann and Beth's interchange illustrated these processes. Their relationship grew and enlarged in the interaction with each other. And
so did each of them.

We are proposing that in reality all people start off with the ability to build mutually empowering relationships. Moreover, despite
the fact that we all have to try to develop within an overriding
dominant-subordinate system, we catch glimpses of mutuality all
around us. We see it in Ann and Beth, in Kathy and Helen, the child
and her mother building with blocks, in men and women, girls and
boys. While we see it particularly in our work with women, we see
it also in those men who transcend or consciously struggle to live
beyond the power-over mode. The men in the group Emerge, in
Cambridge, Massachusetts, offer an example of men working to
build mutual empowerment and counter the effects of patriarchy:
they help wife-batterers try to learn that they can change their violent behavior.

All of this talk of movement in relationship toward mutual empowerment may sound overly idealistic, but that is because patriarchal systems have given us a skewed view of relationships, one that

leads people to think of relationships as restricting rather than as the source of active, creative engagement that enlarges us all.

Further, as women as a group have had the task of providing empathy and engagement for everyone, this activity has not only been insufficiently recognized and described, it has been devalued along with the women who do it. It is therefore something most men would not concentrate on; in fact, if a man did, he might run the risk of being made to feel deviant. For the most part, our culture has not built on this activity as a basis of its thinking, its institutions, or its ways of operating. All of this has led to the diminution and misunderstanding of relational possibilities.

We do not think in terms of the individual versus the relationship, nor of the individual emerging out of relationships, underlying notions that are often at the root of even other relational theorists' thinking. Nor do we think of being in relationship as anything like "dependency," as that word is usually used. Even the word "interdependent" does not capture our meaning; derived as it is from "dependent," it does not convey the *active* participation necessary in creating growth-fostering interplay. Except perhaps for certain hermits, people are always *in* relationships — in schools, workplaces, and organizations, as well as in families — and it's the question of whether these relationships are mutually beneficial or not that is central to our approach.

As Judith Jordan writes, "We are suggesting a . . . rearrangement of traditional theories of 'self-development' when we propose a model of 'relational development' where the 'enhancement of relationship' may constitute a greater goal than individual gratification and ironically may lead to greater individual fulfillment."[16]

GRATIFICATION, DISCONNECTION, AND VIOLENCE

As we have suggested, it makes sense that a dominant group would think in terms of whether it is getting enough gratification from those who are supposed to do the gratifying. (This is essentially the colonizer's style.) Jordan has suggested that we can think about relationships in terms of an empathic-love mode or a power-control mode.[17] An empathic mode would lead people to actively participate together to create mutually enhancing relationships. A power-control mode becomes linked with a focus on whether one can get others to gratify oneself. It readily leads to a sense of entitlement, and from entitlement the step to violation of others is not a long one.

Violation of another represents the opposite of empathy. If one person is empathic to another, s/he will not engage in the kind of disconnection or mistreatment that hurts or violates that person — and violates the relationship. By definition, then, a dominant group cannot encourage empathy in its members or it could not remain dominant; rather, such groups encourage in their members a belief that they are entitled to gratification, to get what they think they need.

With regard to nonmutual relationships, we believe there is a continuum that starts with a lack of awareness of the experience of others and the sense of a person's "right" to coerce them, and at its extreme leads to racial, class, or other oppressions on the societal level, and on the more personal level to emotional, physical, and sexual abuse.

Until the last ten to fifteen years, we did not acknowledge how profoundly and extensively this violence pervaded our most intimate relationships. Only with the emergence of the women's movement has the courageous work of many survivors, and then of mental health professionals and academics, revealed the widespread existence of incest and the sexual and physical abuse of women and children. Often still working against strong opposition from within and beyond the professions, these survivors and their allies have brought to light how large is the number of women who are battered — or killed — by their husbands or male partners and how large a number of girls are sexually or physically abused, most often by male family members. As more data are acquired, we are learning that boys are also at risk of sexual as well as physical abuse.

These revelations should have sent shock waves through the mental health professions for several reasons (these professions used to teach that incest occurred once or twice in a million patients). We now know that many forms of psychological suffering have their origins in such trauma combined with the kinds of distressed family relations in which the trauma occurs. This includes many forms of depression, addictions, eating problems, anxiety, self-injurious behavior, suicide attempts, and physical symptoms. It is important to say that all of these problems can occur in people who have not been sexually or physically abused.[18] Further, it is stunning to note how often clinicians had blamed many of these problems on the mother–infant relationship without the recognition of this widespread abuse, most often perpetrated by men. Such blame was supported by a system based on power relationships rather than mutuality.

THE MOTHER–INFANT RELATIONSHIP IN A POWER–OVER CULTURE

It may sound unusual to contrast these two seemingly so disparate phrases. But because it has been so prominent, we want to add a note on the longstanding tendency within the psychodynamic field to see the mother–child relationship, and especially the mother–infant relationship, as the lone cause of almost all psychological (and social) problems. Even some forms of family therapy, which spoke in terms of seeing the whole family as a system, ended in finding that the trouble lay in the "enmeshed mother" or the like.

We believe that this trend has been so popular because it leads away from an analysis of the ways in which the misuse of power operates in our society and how our culture affects the family. A projection of the cause of every problem (and especially some of our seemingly most insoluble and profound problems) back to infancy acts to obscure the workings of a social system that allows deeply destructive disconnections and violations of people, especially but not only women and children, at all ages of life. To blame everything on the mothers of infants discourages a more profound analysis of the intersection of the political, the social, and the psychological.

It is true that some people have their most intense relationships

with their mothers. But this is because mothers are often left to provide the whole relational context for almost everyone in this culture. We believe that our central problems follow from society's
whole way of operating—a way that does not provide growth-
fostering relationships for everyone at every level, that is, in communities, families, workplaces, schools, and other institutions. All
too often, mothers are the only or the major people left to try to fill
in for the total society; usually their efforts are not supported and
valued but instead are demeaned. Since they cannot fulfill this responsibility alone, many women feel like failures and, indeed, are labeled as such by both immediate family members and society in
general, including mental health professionals who then "help" sons
and daughters "separate" from their mothers.[19]

As we have suggested, the need for relational resonance and responsiveness is so great that when it isn't part of a person's experience
that person's psychological growth may be impaired. All too many
of us have had to look mainly to our mothers to provide this responsiveness, so that when the total society fails us, we turn all our disappointment and anger toward them. The enormous burden of responsibility that mothers have been carrying needs to be shared by
all members of society.

This pattern is intensified in families in which the abuse of
power is most striking, for example, in families in which a father
commits incest with a daughter. Such a father is often very controlling and destructive, undermining the relationship between the
mother and daughter and thereby reinforcing the mother's isolation
along with blaming her for his actions. This relates to the puzzling
phenomenon that children growing up in such families often blame
their mothers for the serious abuse committed by their fathers.
Their perspective is shared by many mental health professionals.

The projection of the cause of every problem back to the
mother–infant relationship has always represented an unprovable
proposition. But the evidence is now mounting against seeking this
as the first or only explanation of psychological distress. The story
of so-called borderline personal disorder offers only one example.
After women unearthed the widespread extent of incest and childhood sexual abuse in this society (and others), it became clear that

many people previously diagnosed "borderline personality disorder" were adult survivors of sexual abuse, most often by male family members.[20] Previously theorists had created formulations that always placed the origin of this problem in the mother–child relationship in early life.[21] In similar fashion, many therapists have traced a number of other problems to mothers who were said to be "unavailable" to the infant, without ever recognizing that some of these mothers and their children were experiencing extreme battering by their male partners (or fathers).

However, beyond these specific issues, the understanding of psychological problems requires deeper analysis of the even more hidden sources of disconnections in nonmutual structures of relationships. The work of Carol Gilligan and her group, on adolescent girls, represents such an analysis. Unlike standard explanations of such problems as depression and eating disorders, which had traced their origins to the mother–infant relationship alone, this new work allows us to see that a more important source of many of these problems may lie in what the culture does to girls at adolescence. As Gilligan shows, at adolescence, girls begin to lose an authentic sense of connection to others, and thereby to themselves, because they cannot find ways to bring themselves into growth-fostering relationships in this culture. This more complete analysis is the kind of original and incisive exploration of the intersection of cultural and psychological sources of disconnection and violation that will lead us to a more profound and complex understanding of psychological problems.[22]

We are suggesting that examining the action of creating together the relationships within which all life activity takes place offers us a more accurate notion of the optimal human condition. And we are saying that psychological problems arise whenever children or adults experience the important disconnections that occur in relationships that are less than optimal. These disconnections follow from the overall operations and values of a culture in which one group of people has more power than another and uses that power in a power-over way. We will be elaborating on this statement throughout this book. (We are talking about psychological origins of problems. There are other causes of problems, for example, neurological and biochemical ones, as well as extraordinary life circumstances such as mass traumata and political torture. Even many of these circumstances are often compounded by disconnections.)

We suggest that the study of how people participate in growth-fostering relationships opens up a vision of human possibilities that has been obscured. If this complex and valuable activity continues to be seen as a minor, personal one and the province of women only, however, then it will always be something that women do for others within a context of subservience rather than mutuality. Women will continue to be oppressed and men to be heavily pressured to proceed along a path centering on individual power and gratification. The violence to which the latter stance often leads will continue, and the structure and institutions of society will not change. We believe that studying women's lives offers us a crucial key to thinking about societal transformation — and that this transformation is essential.

PART TWO

DISCONNECTIONS

4

THE SOURCE OF
PSYCHOLOGICAL PROBLEMS

———

We have been referring to disconnections all along. Now we will pursue them in more depth, since we see them as central to understanding people. Indeed, we see them as the major source of psychological problems, mild or severe. We are defining a disconnection as the psychological experience of rupture that occurs whenever a child or adult is prevented from participating in a mutually empathic and mutually empowering interaction.

Disconnections can be relatively minor. Maria's experience when her father was concerned about her math exam and could not respond to her joy about her part in the play offers an obvious example. Major disconnections occur when a person is abused or attacked. They also occur when the people in the surrounding relational context are repeatedly unresponsive to the child or adult's expression of their experience.

Minor disconnections inevitably occur all through childhood and adult life. They need not lead to serious trouble, especially if a person also has many enlarging connections. Children and adults can withstand and even grow from these small disconnections.

Disconnections can resolve into reconnection — a new and better connection. Two key features are usually necessary to bring this about: 1) one must be able to take some action within the relationship to make one's experience known, and 2) the other people in the relationship must be able to respond in a way that leads on toward a new and better connection. That is, in order for children to try to make their experience known, for example, they must feel a measure of safety and have some belief in their parents' ability to hear and respond to that experience. Without an expectation of safety, it is very hard, especially for children (or any person with less power), to pursue the expression of one's experience after an initial disconnection.

The people who bring about the most serious disconnections and violations of others will also have the most trouble engaging in growth-enhancing interactions about their own behavior. It is true of all of us to varying degrees that when we have been unresponsive or hurtful, we find it difficult to talk about our behavior with the people we've hurt or let down. Most of us have a hard time admitting to our failures or harmful actions. Some people may also be unaware of how they affect others and have a hard time allowing other people to tell them. (Tom demonstrates this lack of awareness.)

Here the factor of power enters. In any relationship in which one person has more power, the danger of harm increases. That person can exert a much greater influence on what happens in an interaction, and he or she will also be less likely to seek mutual engagement. It is much harder for the less powerful person to alter the course of an interaction.

Suppose, however, that in the example in Chapter 3, Maria is able to say to her father, "Don't you care about my play?" Or suppose she doesn't say anything, but the expression on her face changes from joy to disappointment and anger and she steps back from her father. If her father is able to notice and respond to the change in her, he might say something like, "You know, I think I was worried about how you were doing in math and I guess I wasn't paying attention. I really am happy about the play. I'm sorry I didn't let you know right off."

Of course, this response can be valid only if he truly is happy about the play. However, even if he is indifferent, he can still restore some connection if he is able to say, "I want you to be happy and I know the play makes you happy." This would not be as mutual as if he were able to join in Maria's joy more fulsomely and playfully, but it would still be a responsive connection.

The results of this kind of interplay between parents and children are many. One is that the child will learn that from time to time she will experience difficult feelings *with* others. Most important, the child feels an increase in her ability to have an effect on her relationships, that is, to see that what she does has an impact. Parents learn too. Several researchers have recently documented how even very young infants begin to communicate and to regulate their interactions with adults. Their studies have shown how an infant as young as three months old influences the responses of adults. For example, it turns its head to the side, away from the adult, when the adult is being too stimulating, and this leads the (responsive) adult to change her/his activity.[1]

As for parents, most of them feel good when they're able to understand a child's experience and respond to it well. In the revised example, Maria's father, if he did "get it" later even though he was not responsive initially, would enjoy the enlarging feeling of reaching a connection with her. This kind of experience feels empowering for many parents; they feel competent as well as connected when they have been able to be mutual in this way. All children confront parents with the need to "stretch" if they are to respond to the child. From truly engaging with these day-to-day threats of disconnection, parents, too, grow and develop.

In this interchange, both Maria and her father have learned a little more about their feelings. Obviously, this clarification occurs at a different level for the child than for the adult, but they both have learned a little more about how their relationship can encompass disappointment, anger, and other feelings, and about how they both can move the relationship along *in the feelings* to a better sense of connection.

SERIOUS DISCONNECTIONS

To discuss more serious disconnections, we'll start with the example of Ann and Tom. Obviously, we are not suggesting that one such incident between two people will lead to major psychological problems. However, their story can serve to illustrate the processes that lead to troubles, processes that are not always so noticeable, especially if an interaction is seen from only one point of view. These can occur in multiple daily interactions extending over a long time as well as in more gross and obviously destructive situations. It's crucial to note that if disconnection persists over time without a change in direction, it can often be very hard for people to feel that their distress about it is legitimate, since each instance may seem "small," as this episode did to Ann.

We will talk first about the immediate effects of this kind of interaction, and then about what an individual does about it over the course of time — and why. We will attempt to explain how powerful the long-term consequences of disconnection can be and how they can lead to what has been labeled psychopathology. In all that follows, we will be talking about processes that go on largely or wholly outside of conscious awareness.

IMMEDIATE CONSEQUENCES

At the start of her interaction with Tom, Ann was feeling sad and frightened about Emily's illness. Tom did not respond to these feelings but instead told her what to do about Emily, what Emily should do, and what Ann should do for his mother. He could well have thought he was being helpful with these suggestions, but the immediate consequence for Ann is that in addition to her initial fear and sadness, she now feels out of touch with Tom — out of connection.

For the sake of our example, let us assume that Ann's reference to her friend's situation arouses sadness and fear in Tom but that he has not learned much about how to handle these feelings within connections with others; indeed, he becomes angry if someone threatens to evoke them. (Tom's mother is getting older and he is concerned about her health. In addition, he begins to worry about Ann when he hears about her friend's illness.)

As she talks with her husband, Ann begins to experience not only bad feelings, but a confusion of emotions. She is picking up some of Tom's mixture of feelings, including his sadness and fear, but he does not tell her directly that he's sad or afraid. In contrast to what happened with Beth, Tom and Ann's feelings and thoughts can't be "between them" or "with both of them," so it feels to Ann as if they are all hers. This experience is very common; it is also very powerful. Even if Tom could merely say that he was having a hard time, Ann might experience this interaction very differently; if, like Maria's father, Tom could describe part of what was going on in him, some sense of connection could be preserved.

But Ann and Tom cannot engage together with the issue at hand, and this lack of engagement is a most important feature in the development of psychological troubles. When the others cannot respond with some mutuality and some recognition of one's feeling-thoughts, one tends to take on the notion that all of the feelings and all of the difficulties must be one's own.

Further, Ann now feels angry. First she "picks up" Tom's anger, then she becomes angry herself about Tom's unresponsiveness to her feelings. This anger becomes tied to and confused with her other emotions.

Ann is now in greater distress than before. Because she feels so alone, Ann's basic reaction would be to want *even more* to try to connect with Tom. Suppose, again for the sake of example, that when she tries to express some of this to Tom, he becomes openly angry and attacking. (Why are you making such a big deal out of this? Why can't you handle things? Why are you always so preoccupied with your own feelings that you can't even think of my mother's needs? Are you so selfish?) Or perhaps he just withdraws.

In either case, Ann's belief that something is wrong with her deepens because her important feelings have led to such troubles. And if her important feelings are so wrong and bad, *she* must be wrong and bad. Because for Ann, as for all of us, her feeling-thoughts *are* her. As Janet Surrey has commented, a person in Ann's situation feels "If there seems to be such a problem, I must be the problem."[2] Again, Ann feels the problem must be *in her.*[3]

Ann's anger adds to this belief. This kind of unclear anger almost always tends to augment a person's feeling that she or he is wrong and bad. Thus Ann's initial feelings of sadness and fear mix with her confusion and anger, and all of these feelings permeate her sense of what happens when you try to connect with others.

We want to make a distinction here. While sadness and fear are difficult feelings, in Ann's case they probably represent an inevitable response to what is really happening, her friend's serious illness; they can be borne and borne best in connection with other people who can engage with them. Now, however, Ann has moved from feeling sad and fearful to a much more complex, confused mixture of feelings. This is different. It is also not a necessary response to Emily's illness; it is a result of the disconnection in the relationship between Ann and Tom.

Disconnections are often even more powerful in their effects on children. A woman named Liz told us of an experience that occurred when she was five or six years old. Her father's mother had had an exacerbation of her heart disease and was taken to the hospital. After a few days she died. The atmosphere in the family was very bleak and chilling; Liz felt terrible. But no one talked about any of their feelings. As she thought back on this as an adult, she remembered a scene at the dinner table that went something like this:

> *Liz*: Why did Grandma have to go to the hospital?
> *Mother*: Because they said they could help her better there.
> *Liz*: What do they do to you in the hospital?

Mother: Sometimes they give you medicines. And there's other treatments too.

Liz: I get medicines at home.

Mother: Well, sometimes they can give you more — stronger medicines — there.

Liz: We could have given her stronger medicines here.

Father: Can't you stop her from all this talking?

Mother: Liz, don't talk about this anymore now.

Liz: But why did she have to go to that hospital?

Mother: You know, maybe tomorrow we can go to find those nice shoes we talked about.

Liz: Maybe if grandma didn't go to that hospital, maybe she wouldn't have died.

Father: (Slams down his napkin and leaves the table.) I told you to stop talking about this.

Mother: (Goes after father, pursuing him into the next room.) Liz, go to your room now.

Liz remembered this particular scene because it was dramatic, but she thought it represented the way things usually felt in her family. At times her mother was responsive to her, but she always seemed downcast and tense. She never seemed to enjoy or take pleasure in Liz. Instead, Liz felt like "an added trouble" for her mother. Her father was often irritable and sometimes angry. Her mother often seemed to be "running around trying to cater to him" and keep him from erupting, leaving Liz disconnected. Sometimes her mother actively punished Liz for "upsetting" her father.

As a child, then, Liz experienced much of the same sense of disconnection that Ann felt, but she was even more confused. In the episode she described, we can see that she was frightened and unclear about what happened to her grandmother. She was asking questions to try to figure it out. She was also probably trying to figure out why she was feeling so bad about her parents and what was going on with them. When she sought the connections she needed for dealing with all of these feelings, she was made to feel as if something was very wrong with her and with all of her impulses.

The feelings that Ann and Liz experienced are the opposites —

not simple opposites, but intensely confounded opposites — of the good things that flow from growth-enhancing, mutually empowering connections. That is, both Ann and Liz felt less able to take action; more than that, they felt that actions based in their experience led to serious trouble. They had less clarity, less knowledge about themselves and the other person(s). They felt a diminished sense of worth. They experienced a decrease in zest or energy and a diminution of their sense of well-being. Most important, they felt that their actions, feelings, and thoughts led not to connection with others but to a confusing sense of isolation.

We want to call attention to this aspect of disconnection. We believe that *the* most terrifying and destructive feeling that a person can experience is psychological isolation. This is not the same as being alone. It is feeling that one is locked out of the possibility of human connection and of being powerless to change the situation. In the extreme, psychological isolation can lead to a sense of hopelessness and desperation. People will do almost anything to escape this combination of *condemned isolation and powerlessness.*

LONG-TERM CONSEQUENCES

Liz remembers not one but many disconnections like the one we have described. (We will continue with the example of Liz here because the long-term consequences of disconnection can be even more serious for children, but we emphasize again that Ann would suffer the same consequences unless she were able to change the course of her interactions with Tom.) Because Liz now experiences more threatening and more complex feeling-thoughts after each such interaction and longs for connections with others in order to try to deal with them, and because her feelings of aloneness and condemned isolation are so powerful, she will try to make connection with those closest to her in any way possible.

This leads to a process that is all too common in people's lives, one that has long-term consequences. Since she cannot find ways to change the relationships available to her, Liz will attempt to change what she can — herself. Specifically, she tries to alter her inner image of herself and others, her internal image of the nature of the connections between herself and others. She must attempt this alone, since her relationships with her parents preclude doing it in interaction with them. This is a complicated process. In order to twist herself into a person acceptable in unaccepting relationships, Liz will have to move away from and redefine large parts of her experience — the parts she believes are not allowed within the relational context in which she lives.

Liz, then, has seen both her mother and father become angry and disconnect from her (in somewhat different ways) when she tries to express her sad and fearful feelings. She has created the relational image that says that the only way to find connection with her parents is to act on what *they* want. Therefore, because she wants and needs this connection, she tries to act on what she construes to be their feelings and wishes. (She could be wrong about what they feel and think, but she does not have a good way of knowing.) She has "learned" that she cannot express sadness and fear, so she tries to become a person who never has such feelings. She tries to have only what she considers to be good, pleasant, and positive feelings — such as wanting to do what her parents want.

Liz comes to believe she must feel this way at all times in order to have any sort of connection with other people, that others will not tolerate anything but these constricted and unrealistic feelings and expressions. When events occur that cause sadness, fear, anger, or any of the "unacceptable" feelings, she feels upset but cannot be certain what she is experiencing — except that she shouldn't be feeling whatever she's feeling. And her confusion increases her distress. In time, whenever she does feel the possibility of closeness with anyone, she pulls away for fear that she will experience the old, terrible, confused mixture of disappointment, hurt, anger, and isolation. She appears compliant, but she has become ever more disconnected.

It is important to emphasize that while there is initial confusion about many feelings in nonmutual relationships, certain feelings tend to become especially significant over time. One is fear or anxiety. Liz may become increasingly afraid of other people since her relational images lead her to expect that they may evoke the "forbidden" thoughts and feelings. Further, she may become afraid of large portions of her own experience, because she will inevitably experience many emotions that threaten to disrupt the highly controlled images she has formed of herself and others.

One of the most important of these is anger. Anger threatens Liz's image of herself as a person who has only good and loving feelings. Yet no one can undergo long-term disconnections without experiencing serious anger, in addition to that which arises from common everyday causes. Thus anger becomes particularly problematic rather than an emotion that can be valuable in a relationship.[4] As a result of her controlled images, Liz may be confused about anger but may suffer depression, anxiety, or a number of other symptoms instead.

Eventually, Liz will be able to allow herself only limited kinds of relationships since she can tolerate only certain feelings in others as well as in herself. Others must see her as only good and loving, not fearful, sad, or angry, and she must see herself this way, too. To be otherwise is to feel cast out and condemned.

All of these fears about other people or one's own emotions take away from a person's basis for expansion. Liz doesn't have a sense that new feelings, new experience, or new relationships will bring more sense of connection, knowledge, sense of worth, zest, and ability to act. Quite the opposite; she starts to feel that engagements with other people are threatening. And yet, just because of this sense of threat, she deeply needs and wants the connections that can help her deal with all of her difficult feelings.

Over time, a large part of what Liz does and says arises not from the possibilities available in her actual experience within relationships but out of her image of what she believes she must be in order to be allowed into connection with others; much of what she actually does in the world, often very worthy actions, does not connect fully with the truth of her own experience. To the extent that this is so, her actions cannot build her image of herself as worthy; moreover, they cannot alter the inner, increasingly walled-off portion of herself which consists of all her "bad" feelings and thoughts.

DISCONNECTING RELATIONAL IMAGES
AND CONDEMNING MEANINGS

In Chapter 2, we began a discussion of relational images, the inner patterns or models of relationships that we each create out of what's happened to us. These become the key inner concepts we use to order our experience, and they then guide our actions. Once they are established we carry them in us; they become the framework by which we determine who we are, what we can do, and how worthwhile we are.

We have also said that if people have repeated connections like the one between Ann and Beth they will tend to create images that portray relationships as empowering encounters in which they feel heard and understood, hear and understand others, are motivated to act, and feel more worthwhile and more connected. By contrast, we can see that Liz's experiences of disconnection led her to very different images.

It is significant that Ann and Beth were creating relational images informed by their experience together, whereas Liz was left to create hers alone. At a moment of disconnection — at the time they most need it — people don't have the very engagement with other people that is the source of the only possibility of arriving at a more accurate understanding of what is happening.

Most people's relational images are complex, and the process of creating them occurs with varying degrees of awareness; a large part of it may not be conscious.

Relational images are probably built on very early images, beginning in infancy. No one knows what really goes on in the mind of an infant, but researcher Daniel Stern has suggested a description of likely patterns.[5] For example, we can postulate that as a young infant, Liz may have begun to build a pattern that portrayed "This soft warm something feels good whenever it is near," but that as she went on to have more difficult experiences, this image became progressively more complicated: "Every time I try to get near the soft warm thing, something else gets in the way"; "Whenever I get near the soft warm thing, I get angry because something is going to block me"; "Whenever I get near a person who seems warm and loving I get angry, but anger is bad." The initial pattern has now developed into something very different, a condensation of complicated notions.

Relational images continue to develop all through life. People have many different kinds of experience, much of it inconsistent or contradictory, thus they may have confusing sets of images. Most important, people do not just incorporate these patterns passively, they also use them to create ideas about what they can *do* about their experience. If people cannot engage with others about the important events of their lives, they are left to try to figure out what they can or must do all on their own.

From her experience as traced above, Liz has created the image that she can find relationships only if she conforms to what other people want; if she does not, they will attack and/or abandon her. She may not be fully conscious of her images, but she tries to find ways to avoid getting near a person who is warm and loving so that this chain of events will not occur. She may appear to be distant, but under it all she deeply longs for a relationship with an emotionally giving person; however, she has moved a long way from knowing and acting on that longing. She may try to achieve this connection not by asking for anything directly but by trying to conform to what she thinks others demand, while holding herself aloof and not truly connected to them.

People devise a great many variations on such "solutions" — responses to disconnection — many of which, ironically, perpetuate disconnections in future interactions. If their available relationships are, on balance, restrictive and hurtful, they have to do much of this creating alone, as Liz had to do, without the benefit of the kind of clarifying and enlarging interchange that Ann and Beth illustrated. As Liz goes through life, if she does not have other people who can engage with her, her images can become increasingly "confirmed," even quite fixed and difficult to alter. As a result, she may create a much more limited set of possibilities than is necessary. Even in a society that discourages mutual relationships, there are sometimes more possibilities than one is able to construe on one's own.

As they are developing relational images, people are also constructing a set of beliefs about *why* their relationships are the way they are. These constructions provide the *meanings* of relational images and have implications about the individual, about others, and about relationships. Like the images they are based on, these meanings don't necessarily reflect the total situation accurately. In fact, Liz had a father who was exploited on his job and in turn dominated his family. He was usually irritable, angry, and unable to be empathic with his daughter's or his wife's experience. Liz's mother was depressed and preoccupied with her husband's anger. Neither parent was able to respond well to Liz. One of Liz's relational images was the picture of herself trying to convey her experience and nobody wanting to hear her; her accompanying constructions then included a belief that she must not be worthy of connection since no one seemed to have an interest in her thoughts and feelings. It is not true that she was unworthy. As is the case with many people (some of whom we will describe in Chapter 5), Liz's parents were inaccessible as well as unresponsive to her. Their inaccessibility made it hard for her to find out *why* they couldn't respond to her. As a result, she could not form accurate relational images either about them or about herself.

At the most basic and pervasive level, Liz created constructions of herself as the deficient, defective, or blameworthy person. As we described earlier, because Liz's most important relationships had been characterized by disconnections, she believed she must be the problem.

Typically, people who have experienced significant disconnections create meanings that assign blame to themselves. As disconnections recur — and, most important, as people cannot find ways to engage with others about these disconnections — their sense of condemnation intensifies. Thus, they will "explain" all of the relational images that portray disconnections in any form by the construction that they are deeply undesirable or even malevolent. In our experience, even a person who may be vociferous and adamant about her/his parent's or other people's faults, harbors, at bottom, the devastating pain of believing that s/he is really the worthless one.

Many features feed into making these constructions so self-condemning. When people experience serious disconnections or violations, it is often so painful and frightening that they cannot bear to stay right in the experience fully and go through all of the pain and fear. Instead, they feel impelled to move immediately out of the experience, and therefore they do not have the chance to create more accurate and complex constructions about what is happening and why. They cannot stay with the mixture of feelings and find ways to sort out, understand, clarify, and integrate the experience as Ann and Beth were able to do. At the time of disconnection, there is no one who can engage with them about what is occurring, and so the experience is usually deeply confusing.

As a result of such confusion, people leap to some sort of construction that will explain their experience. Because the overriding motivation is to stay in connection, the explanation must be one that will allow them to fit in with the very people who are preventing an empathic and empowering connection. Liz felt frightened and confused about what had happened to her grandmother and also about the unexpressed feelings in her family. When she tried to ask about what was going on, she was made to feel disconnected and alone. In her aloneness with these feelings, she devised explanations which meant she was "bad."

We have traced above how both Ann and Liz initially felt that they were wrong to have the feelings they did. In our clinical practice we see many women who have had similar experiences, and all too often, the more hurt or violated a person is made to feel, the more she leaps to the belief that she is the bad one. Nancy, whose father sexually abused her, felt she must be a profoundly malevolent person if her father was treating her this way. Yet she knows another truth — that is, she experienced the disconnection and the pain.

At the time that all of us create many of the meanings of our most basic relational images — as children and in the context of our families — we are not yet mature enough to understand the complexities of relationships. Our earliest and most basic constructions are likely to be simple and absolute. Liz's father was caught in his job and his anger, and her mother was caught in her fear and depression; that did not mean that Liz was an undesirable person, but she could not know that. As a child, she could not be aware of these facts, let alone begin to fathom what economic conditions or psychological depression can do to people. Instead, she drew from her parents' inability to engage with her the meaning that she was unworthy.

People construct self-disparaging meanings when they do not have enough possibilities for mutual engagement within their families. Further, if they have no alternative sources of connection outside of their families to help them form a better picture of the reasons for their experience, these meanings will persist. As we will see in Chapters 5 and 6, some kinds of families render children particularly isolated from other people, but in our culture all children are isolated to some degree.

Children create these constructions when they are the least powerful people in the relationship, with the least possibility of altering it in ways that would allow them to find new relational images and hence new constructions. Moreover, once they begin to feel unworthy, it becomes harder to move toward other possible relationships even if they may be available — that is, to find other people who could be more responsive. Self-disparaging constructions thus become the source of profound and continuing "internalized oppression."

Liz carried within her into adulthood the belief that she was a deeply unworthy person. As a child and then as an adult, she held people off and kept herself much more isolated from relationships outside the family than she needed to be. She herself had constructed meanings that oppressed her.

While the constructions created in childhood are powerful, adults continue to create new constructions and to elaborate upon and revise prior ones. In times of major disconnections, adults, too, can create self-blaming meanings. For example, women who have been raped or battered often come to believe deep down that they are themselves unworthy, and even blameworthy, because of the abuse they have suffered.

Battered women have described this as a spiraling process. The more they are mistreated, the more worthless and ashamed they feel, and the more they withdraw from other people. Not only does a batterer often actively insist on keeping the woman isolated, she herself creates over time constructions about her own unworthiness and augments her own isolation. Similarly, women who've been raped often become convinced they were at fault.

More commonly, many women create self-denigrating constructions when they are caught in relationships with partners or other important figures who fail to respond to their experience. For instance, Ann might form such a construction if her interactions with her husband repeatedly took the course they did in our vignette.

We used the example of Ann and Tom, adults, because we want to emphasize that disconnections can cause significant troubles at *any* time of life. Certainly, one incident with a spouse does not lead to serious psychological problems, but repeated experiences of disconnection can, especially if one is not able to find a way to change the course of the interaction. We have seen many women whose depressions, anxiety states, phobias, and other problems are clearly related to their current relationships — women whose depressions and other symptoms reflect deep disappointment in current relationships much more than they reflect failures in their early relationships with their mothers, as traditional theory would have it.[6] We have also seen such symptoms diminish and a woman's total way of being change if she can find the ways to alter the relationship in question. The same improvement occurs if she finds other connections that empower her to take action and to leave the destructive situation. Carolyn Swift describes how new connections with other women, for example, can enable a woman to leave a battering relationship.[7]

Of course, the whole process of disconnection and self-denigration runs much deeper if it begins in childhood. In addition to having less ability to understand the relationships within the family and less power to change these conditions, the child is also trapped. A child cannot leave.

But while these constructions of meaning can become very deep-seated, they can also change, as we will illustrate. A person can come to understand his or her relational images differently. Finding these different meanings can change our convictions about ourselves and enlarge our beliefs about the possibilities open to us. Psychotherapy is one path to this transformation. Other kinds of growth-fostering relationships in life can also open up new relational images and meanings.

While we have been describing the construction of self-deprecating meanings, it is important to remember that people also create other relational images and constructions that provide a sense of worth. Often people have constructed a mixture of various relational images and accompanying meanings, and sometimes these may be contradictory and confusing.

THE CENTRAL RELATIONAL PARADOX

As Liz builds increasingly restrictive relational images and meanings, she continues to seek connections but she can do so only by keeping more and more of her experience and her reactions to her experience out of these connections. We see this process as *the central relational paradox*, and we believe it is basic to understanding many psychological problems. It is also basic to understanding therapy for these problems, as we will describe in later chapters.

In keeping large parts of herself out of connection, Liz cannot relate fully to other people in the ways that lead to growth. Thus the parts of herself that she has excluded are unable to change from experience. Her continuous construction of a sense of herself and of others cannot be enlarged by the interchange within connections, which is precisely the source of the clarity and knowledge needed for the development of an increasingly accurate image of oneself and others. Liz is forming inner images of relational possibilities — and impossibilities — with less and less actual learning from action within relationships. These inner images then limit her feelings, thoughts, and action in all realms.

This path away from mutual connection, and simultaneously away from the truth of one's own experience, is the path to psychological problems. We believe it underlies many of the problems common to women in particular, including depression, various forms of anxiety, phobias, eating problems, and the so-called personality disorders, such as "borderline personality."

Each of these has its particular features, and in the next chapter we will discuss some of these particularities, but in our view, all of these problems grow out of the attempt to find a possibility of acting within connection when the only connections available present major impossibilities — when the available relational contexts involve disconnections or even violations of one's experience.

It is striking to note that Carol Gilligan's group has arrived at a formulation of a paradox that is almost identical. We have suggested that the contradiction inherent in keeping large parts of one's experience and responses out of connection in order to try to find connections is central to many psychological troubles. Gilligan and her colleagues have contributed a powerful body of work that shows us how this occurs in a particularly intense way for girls at adolescence. Girls who have been active, direct, multifaceted, and confident — and especially those who have been keen observers of relationships — begin to talk and act differently; they appear to lose certain lively and important parts of themselves, especially their abilities to understand and comment on what they see around them, as they try to fit into the kinds of relationships that the culture prescribes for them; they "go underground." As Gilligan articulates it, this is a paradox that all women in this culture face, one with profound effects on the possibilities for their psychological development.[8]

Sexual and physical abuse represent an extreme but all too frequent illustration of the disconnection and silencing of girls and women — and of boys and men as well. When physically or sexually abused, a person is violated psychologically as well and will usually be unable to represent the truth of this experience either within the immediate relational context or in a larger one.

These forms of violence represent the most severe form of the psychological violation and disconnection that can occur whenever one person (or group of people) has greater power to define what can and cannot occur within relationships. Here is the complete opposite of the search for mutually empowering connections.

In this chapter, we've suggested that a relational context that includes serious or repeated disconnections will lead people to create restricted and distorted images of the possibilities of relationships between themselves and others, and to construct meanings that disparage and condemn themselves. These images and meanings then further limit their ability to act within connections, to know their own experience and to build a sense of worthiness.

We've suggested that girls and women who are sexually violated experience an extreme form of a process that occurs for most women — indeed, we believe, for everyone. Women who are sexually violated and the women who work with them are teaching us today perhaps the most important things we need to learn in order to fathom the hidden aspects of psychological development, not only of girls and women but also of boys and men, who are developing within a societal context that allows such widespread violence.

In our discussion of the origins of psychological troubles, we've drawn upon the thinking of many schools of thought, including Freudians, object relations theorists, self psychologists, and the work of Horney, Sullivan, and Rogers.[9] But we have not used terms such as "false selves" or "true selves," which follow from a focus on the self and the question of how it is built and strengthened or weakened.

Instead, using language common to us all, we've tried to explore what happens when we take women seriously, when their experiences come to life, because (though this is obvious, it's rarely stated) it is mainly women who have been made into "objects" in all of these theories. As such, they supply the material by which the "subjects" build systems of selves and the like.

When women enter the picture as persons, we move inevitably to different assumptions. We then cannot proceed on the premise of a self that is using "objects" in order to develop more of a self. Rather than asking, What strengthens a self? we ask, What supports mutuality? What leads to disconnection?

5

HOW DISCONNECTIONS
HAPPEN IN FAMILIES

In this chapter we will identify some of the conditions that lead to major disconnections within families.

To begin with, in a situation of nonmutuality, the most profound consequence for an individual is a deep sense of disconnection and isolation — precisely the feelings that then lead to the development of psychological troubles. These troubles can exist for almost everyone living in this society. Farther along on the same continuum are even more serious problems, and these are also common.

Two vignettes illustrate how the central relational paradox we've described plays out in the context of even subtle power inequities within the family.

Carol, the mother of two small boys, had decided that she wanted to stay home when she had children. She came from a blue-collar family, and her mother had worked outside the home all her life to help support the family. Carol wanted to do things differently; however, she often felt bored at home and would become frustrated and angry with her children, who were very active and competitive with each other. In the late afternoon she would begin to feel the need for her husband to come home, to talk to her, to listen to her grievances. Yet as soon as he entered the house he would attend to his mail and then make phone calls or turn on the television to watch the news. She felt her husband was very much the center of her life, yet she saw how far she was from being the center of his, and how little he participated in the life of the family.

Carol tried to persuade herself that he needed to unwind when not at work, but she became increasingly "difficult" and argumentative. She felt that other family members, her own relatives and her in-laws, saw her as someone who added to her husband's burdens. Her mother always reminded her of what a good life she had with this successful and reliable husband. In growing up, she had seen her mother always deferring to her father. For example, her mother's letters were replete with phrases such as "your father thought," "your father said," "your father would like," which irritated Carol; yet she felt there was no reason for her irritation since her father was "more practical" than her mother.

This situation demonstrates the central relational paradox. Carol made intense efforts to maintain her relationship with her husband and children, but because of power differentials and a lack of mutuality she did so by negating much of her own experience when it conflicted with her husband's expectations and wishes.

Carol believed she was in a reasonably good marriage. Although sometimes critical of both of her parents, she did not feel that her family history was troublesome. She was trying to adapt to a relationship that was nonmutual, one in which she did not feel the legitimacy of her own needs. Furthermore, she did not feel able to even begin to engage with her husband about her feelings. She couldn't venture into the kind of exploration that might lead to more clarity and action within the relationship. She was attempting to maintain the relationship by leaving important parts of herself out of it, and as a result she stayed out of authentic connection. She felt disconnected from the very person she so wanted to value her.

The power differentials that characterize our patriarchal society are evident, at different levels, in all our family, work, and social settings. Whether both partners work outside the home or not, Carol's marriage was typical in many respects; in fact, public opinion might judge it to be better than many. Yet she did not experience the man in her life as truly empathic with her experience; instead she blamed herself for not being sufficiently empathic with her husband's experience. Certainly the readiness with which women blame themselves (or their mothers) for their sad and angry feelings reflects the expectations in the broader cultural context that those with less power (women) accommodate to those who have more power, in order to have any relationship at all. Thus, many women do not expect true mutuality in their relationships (even though they yearn for it). Consequently, they do not recognize the legitimacy of their pain and distress when the important people in their lives do not sufficiently acknowledge, resonate, and respond to their experiences.

This is an example of one woman who did not feel she could more fully represent herself in her relationship with her husband and in the end believed that she was being unreasonable to expect more from her marriage. The dynamics of the central relational paradox can be seen at work in other kinds of relationships when power inequities lead to a lack of mutuality, such as relationships between parent and child, or employer and employee.

The experience of Mary, a thirty-eight-year-old woman, illustrates how a seemingly mutual relationship between a parent and child can break down in the face of a conflict between them. Mary was married, and very successful in her work, receiving more and more recognition over the years. Her father had always been supportive, encouraging her to go to graduate school and to pursue her career. She felt very close to him and knew that he took pride in her success.

After receiving an important promotion with increased obligations and responsibilities, she began to bring work home evenings and weekends. Her marriage had been troubled for some years, a fact she had not shared with her parents because she didn't want to worry them. Although she thought her husband was a caring person, he was quite remote and she often felt frustrated and angry by his lack of responsiveness to her concerns and feelings. Also, he was much less successful at work than she, and she was often reluctant to share her pleasure in her own achievements with him, lest he feel bad and inadequate about his own career. She had hoped that the gratification she received from the work itself and from her professional relationships would balance her loneliness and disappointment in her marriage.

However, her relationship with her husband became increasingly problematic. She felt she could no longer avoid facing the seriousness of the situation and decided to talk to her parents about these marital difficulties. Her father became enraged. He told her the recent promotion had been too much, that she was putting her job ahead of her family and her husband should come first, that if she stopped all this nonsense and put her energies into her marriage rather than her work, things would be different and better. She was devastated. Her father's reaction was unexpected, but it confirmed her worry that her personal life was compromised by her getting ahead in her career.

Although Mary was at some level shocked at her father's response, she also realized that she had always known that his support of her career was conditional, that he valued her accomplishments as long as she was a "good wife" and a "dutiful daughter." Growing up, she had seen her father's outbursts of anger toward her mother when her mother was not available and responsive to him. Her mother started a business of her own when Mary was an adolescent, and became quite successful. Her father changed jobs frequently and earned less money than her mother, but he had prestigious titles in the positions he held. Mary was aware that the family myth was that her father was the successful, serious worker, while her mother was doing things to "keep her busy." Still, she had felt more connected with her father and experienced her mother as very demanding and critical.

After the encounter with her father, Mary saw how much she

had always played down her successes at work with her husband and friends, and how much she had been afraid to share with her father. She could not acknowledge to him how lonely she was in her marriage, nor how much her work really meant to her. She became aware that she had always told him about the rewards, the "prizes," not the meaning of the work itself.

What are the consequences of such accommodations? We recognize in these two vignettes small or large signs of the ways in which women often seem troubled, angry, and depressed in relationships that may seem on the surface to be fairly positive. These women often feel there is no legitimacy to their disappointments and painful feelings, and, as a result, they learn not to express — and sometimes not even to know — those aspects of themselves that seem to threaten the important relationships in their lives.

Carol longed to be important to her husband in the way he was to her. When she saw that this was not possible, she hid her disappointment but became a person criticized and blamed by both her family and her in-laws for "wanting too much." This certainly had an impact on her self-worth and left her feeling further disconnected and alone.

Mary longed to engage with her family as she truly was, that is, as a woman of talent and achievement, but felt judged and at risk of disconnection from both her father and her husband because of her success in her career. She believed that if she more fully represented that part of herself that so enjoyed what she did in her work and the recognition she received, she might distress or displease the important people in her life. In the end, she stayed out of authentic connection with both her parents and her husband and experienced herself with them as "bad wife" and "bad daughter."

These vignettes describe some consequences of nonmutual relationships between adults. The potential for developing psychological difficulties is significantly increased when children, who are the most powerless members of families, consistently experience relationships that are not responsive to their experience, that negate the legitimacy of their longings, or that preclude their understanding of what is happening around them.

In order to explore how more severe psychological difficulties can evolve in these settings, we need to describe what kinds of circumstances lead to significant systematic disconnections. We have to look at what actually happens in those families in which children are unable to represent themselves and come to feel more deeply isolated and even condemned. They share some common, salient features.

NONMUTUAL PATTERNS IN FAMILIES

Three prominent features or patterns emerge from and perpetuate nonmutual family relationships and chronic disconnections among family members: (1) secrecy in the family, or what is sometimes referred to as a conspiracy of silence, to deny an "unacceptable" reality; (2) inaccessibility of the parents, so that the children have neither permission nor the opportunity to learn and know about them; (3) "parentification" of children, which occurs when children are placed prematurely in positions of responsibility that are not reciprocated.

These (and other) patterns have been recognized by mental health professionals, but they have not been understood as examples of what we see as a basic human problem — disconnection.

When parents in a family cannot construct a mutual relationship in which they can deal with the important issues in their lives, they tend to fall into constrictive patterns. As these patterns become more and more consolidated, both parents tend to sustain them, feeling unable to find any other. Thus both parents tend to become caught up in keeping them going once they're begun.

Secrecy

Every family has its share of secrets. However, the destructive effects of secrecy are most apparent in those families that are energetically organized to maintain silence about issues that are of central importance on a day-to-day basis.

Extreme situations dramatically illustrate the consequences of power inequities and the profound disconnections that are experienced by all family members. For example, in a family in which incest occurs, the conspiracy of silence is essential to the continuation of the incestuous relationship. The perpetrator may cajole, threaten, terrorize, or victimize the child. While some family members may be unaware of what has been happening, others may know at least "something" but maintain the secrecy and denial in order to hold on to some connection with the abuser and with one another. Characteristically, the person exercises extreme control over all family members so that contacts with people outside the family are minimal and dependency on each other is intensified.[1]

Secrecy in such a family serves to bond the abuser and the victim — most often father and daughter — together through terror and compliance, thereby isolating the child further from other relational possibilities. The terror of exposure and the enormous guilt and shame a child experiences keep her silent and isolated from her peers and from adults outside the family. Many adult children from incestuous families continue throughout life to have difficulty talking about anything personal or speaking "the truth." One woman, entering a group of other incest survivors with much trepidation, said, "I have the sensation that just as I am ready to talk a clamp comes over my mouth." Another said, "If I speak about it I'll betray my family."[2]

Even when a family secret is much less destructive, it can still create disconnections among all family members. Those who know cannot relate authentically to those from whom the secret must be kept; those shut out of the secret feel cut off and disconnected. For example, a woman we'll call Amy entered therapy because she became depressed after her divorce. But what became apparent very early on was that she was more distressed about the many things her husband had kept from her over the twelve years of their marriage than about the divorce itself. She learned that he had never told her about a previous marriage or about a son from that marriage with whom he had maintained an important relationship over the years, though their children knew about these things. Amy suffered not only from the loss of her husband, but from the loss of a relationship that she now felt had never existed; she felt completely cut off from the years she and her husband had spent together and deeply estranged from her children.

Amy's sense of disconnection from her husband and her children was profound in its own right, but in the course of therapy it also brought to light another secret — one from her own family of origin. It wasn't until she was sixteen that she learned from a family friend that she had had a brother who'd died in a drowning accident a year before she was born. Neither parent had ever mentioned him. When she confronted her mother with this new knowledge, her mother was so overwhelmed with sadness that Amy didn't feel she could ever bring it up again. But Amy's mother did tell her that her brother had drowned in a backyard pool after the mother had entered the house to take a phone call. She begged her daughter not to bring it up with her father, who "could not bear it." Amy then became the "holder" of a secret to be kept from her father. She felt cut off from her mother, with a mixture of rage and sadness because her mother had never told her about her brother and yet was suffering so much. She felt even more cut off from her father, with whom she could not engage about the topic at all.

Over the course of therapy it became apparent to Amy that the secret of her brother's existence had organized almost all facets of her life. She became aware that she had probably had some awareness of the secret before she was told it explicitly, in that she had felt she was never able to be the kind of child she believed her parents would have preferred her to be. This sometimes took the form of the fantasy that if she were a boy she could have made her father happy, or that if only she weren't such a tomboy her mother would not be so worried and always angry with her. Amy had, indeed, been very accident-prone as a youngster. Her mother would become furious when Amy sustained injuries, leaving Amy feeling "bad" and alone, or intensely involved with her care after an accident, making Amy feel more guilty than cared for.

Once she was "in on" the secret, Amy tried to find ways to fill the gap left by the lost brother, by marrying someone whom she felt would be "like a son" to her father but whom she really did not love herself, and by creating opportunities for her sons to develop a relationship with her parents — which both sons were resistant to do.

In all areas of her life Amy did not feel free to represent herself truly, and she felt despair about ever making a difference or having an impact on the important people in her life. She realized how much she had lived under a cloud of expectation that something terrible would befall the people she loved. Amy's family illustrates dramatically how two parents could not deal with their feelings together, with serious consequences for their daughter.

Sometimes a family secret is not identified as such but family members are in collusion in not recognizing a significant piece of reality; the repercussions are often similar to those that are evoked by more explicit secrets. Edith, a woman who was the daughter of an alcoholic, recalled that every evening after supper her father would sit down in front of the TV and begin drinking until he was comatose; no one in her family ever mentioned it or alluded to her father at all in this setting. She herself learned not to notice, not to "see" a significant reality in her household. Yet she believed all the other members of her family must understand more of what was going on around her.

Only years later, in therapy, did she make a connection between this situation and her inability to "see the whole picture" in other categories, including in a variety of jobs. This apparent "blindness" significantly limited her ability to solve problems and to succeed. She also became aware of how much she held herself back from close relationships. She always felt humiliated when others saw things more clearly than she did. She felt there must be something wrong with her since she didn't understand or "see" what others noticed. She also believed that her feelings and point of view in a relationship were too insignificant to be communicated to others. She had developed the relational image that what she saw and felt was not important and that others would not like to hear what she had to say.

In some instances the "secret" is known by everyone but not explicitly acknowledged and thus cannot be discussed openly nor fully understood. A woman named Lisa had always known that her mother was Jewish, but it was also clear to Lisa that her father did not want this fact mentioned, and her mother never volunteered it. Her mother's parents had died a few years before her marriage to Lisa's father, and Lisa's mother had joined the church her husband belonged to although she never went to services. Lisa sensed her father's wish to keep her mother's Jewishness hidden, and she realized that it contributed to her sense of shame about both her own and her mother's heritage. She came to see how much both she and her mother had kept large parts of themselves out of connection both with each other and with Lisa's father.

Despite the different details of these examples, the dynamics and consequences are similar. In particular, there are significant power inequities between those who "know" the secret and those who must be shut out. Secrets interfere with the development of authenticity and relational capabilities. Parents and other family members cannot "see" or acknowledge fully what they actually know at some level. They become blind to or deflect communications which may threaten to lead them to emotions associated with the secrets they are keeping. For example, Amy's parents could not share with her any experience of fear or sadness. Children experience a deep sense of hopelessness and helplessness when they cannot have an impact on their parents, when they feel unseen and unheard by them. In such situations, there is little opportunity for children to share experiences and to gain greater clarity of thought and self-knowledge in the process.

Secrecy also deeply affects the development of feelings of worth or self-esteem. As we know, when children are aware of some discrepancy between their perceptions and what they are told, they typically will blame themselves for the discomfort they feel and for not seeing "right."

Finally, secrecy isolates children from the world. That is, the danger and fear of others finding out, and the taboo about talking to people outside the family lest this happen, disempower children from acting in the world and from moving out of the family for support. In the family, relationships are so conditional on maintaining a myth that authentic interactions are impossible. Thus, the key result of secrecy is a denial of external reality *and* of inner experience. The conspiracy of silence requires all family members to collude to maintain some semblance of connection, but in the process all members are kept out of relationship, disconnected from one another and from their own experience.

Inaccessibility of Parents

Secrecy certainly interferes with parents' accessibility, and inaccessibility conveys a powerful message to children that people cannot present to others who they truly are, nor tell the truth about their experiences in life. Thus, children are prevented from taking the first basic step into mutually empathic relationships. Although families may differ in the reasons for parents' inaccessibility, and also in the ways in which this is experienced by the children, the result in most families is that the children feel unable to have an impact on their parents and feel shut out of genuine engagement with them.

When parents are too preoccupied, too split off, too much compelled by their own needs, or too depleted to be responsive to their children and to their children's need to know their parents, and when they are unable to share their own experiences or family histories, the children will feel cut off from both their own emotions and other family members.

Inaccessibility of parents contributes to a climate in which the child feels shut out of others' experience on a day-to-day basis and at a loss in trying to understand what is happening. Such a climate serves to intensify the child's feelings of helplessness, of not being able to "figure out" how to have an impact on her/his parents in ways that can lead to feeling connected with them and empowered in the world.

An all too common kind of inaccessibility can be seen in the families of alcoholics. The alcoholic parent is, of course, most inaccessible when drunk. Children growing up in these families talk about the confusion and anxiety aroused by the apparent presence of their alcoholic parent when he or she is not truly present at all. Even in the best of circumstances, that is, when the alcoholic is neither violent nor unpleasant, he or she will often not recall what transpired, will make promises that will be denied later, and will be incapable of genuine and consistent emotional expression.

A woman whose father was an alcoholic stated, "I never know who it is I am responding to. . . . There are so many different personalities: the sober father, the drunk father, the father who is so tense when he's trying to stay off the booze." Another woman said,

"I was perplexed by my father's personality changes and wondered how he could always act like nothing out of the ordinary happened the morning after."[3] How difficult it must be to get any sense of "knowing about" a parent who changes personality style so dramatically and in such an unpredictable fashion. And how powerless the child must feel in attempting to engage with such a parent in any genuine and mutual fashion.

The alcoholic drinks, in part, to become emotionally numb, in order not to feel. This typically renders the alcoholic either barely present at all (comatose or nonreactive) or explosive and rageful. These feelings are dissociated and later forgotten. Children growing up in alcoholic families talk about being unable to trust that the feelings their parents express to them will be consistent and "real" — and about how hard it is for them to know or trust the reality of their own feelings. Indeed, it can be terrifying to risk an expression of genuine feeling if one expects that the other person will not acknowledge it, and instead will disengage and disconnect.

In families where a parent suffers from depression, children also experience that parent as inaccessible and unknown to them. We know that depression is much more prevalent in women than men, and that there are many children who grow up with depressed mothers. Certainly there is a continuum of degree, but any level of depression can be disconnecting and isolating. This is particularly so when a depressed mother is very withdrawn, retreats to her bedroom for days, and cannot mobilize the energy to engage with her children or assume responsibilities at home or work. Typically, children of a depressed parent feel it is their fault, that they are the cause of the parent's unhappiness, and they feel guilty about the obvious pain and distress they see the parent experiencing. Because depressed parents are so often preoccupied, disengaged, and unable to explain what is happening, their children have no way to make sense out of the profound disconnection they are experiencing.

A woman named Louise described a very close relationship with her mother in growing up. She also remembers adoring her father when she was a small child and that he was playful and loving. But over the years her father's alcoholism led him to become more absent and unavailable. Her mother began to confide in Louise about her disappointment in the marriage and periodically became very depressed. During these depressive episodes, Louise's father would disappear for days and she would feel totally responsible for helping her mother feel better. When her mother was depressed she would become irritable and seclude herself in her bedroom, and Louise would feel abruptly cut off. This experience of disconnection was particularly exacerbated when Louise's mother underwent electroshock therapy; when she came home after one of these treatments she was often very confused, her face looked blank, and she was unresponsive.

Over the years Louise became more and more isolated. She discovered that when she did make efforts to engage in some social interaction she would become "sick to her stomach," which further entrenched her isolation. (She was later able to connect this feeling to how she had felt when her mother came back from an electroshock treatment.) She began to value solitude, insisting that she was much more content when alone than with people, and turned to books and music as her companions.

Over the course of therapy, she gradually began to move out of isolation and to start several warm relationships with women colleagues at work. She realized, however, that she could not believe that these women genuinely liked her and that she was always anticipating that at any moment they would lose interest in her and cut her off. This kept her from engaging more fully with them and allowing the relationships to grow.

As Louise explored these feelings in therapy, she became acutely aware of how much of an impact her parents' inaccessibility had had on her understanding of all relationships. When her father drank he became a totally different person from the father who seemed to love her; she could not understand who he really was and she expected less and less of him through the years. Similarly, when her mother became depressed, Louise could not recognize her as the mother who at other times was able to relate to her, and she could not understand what was happening to her mother.

We have said that when there is a significant lack of mutuality between parents, certain patterns of disconnection develop. In our patriarchal society, women are particularly disappointed by a lack of mutuality in their marital relationships and they often express their unhappiness in ways that limit their accessibility to children and other family members. One woman, describing how unavailable her own mother was while she was growing up, said that her primary memory of her was that her mother was always at home, very occupied, and that whenever one of the children approached her she would invariably say, "Not now. I'm busy."

In addition, in families in which there are secrets or parents are emotionally inaccessible — or both — the past is often idealized, largely as a function of the picture the family attempts to present to the community. The children learn not to ask about a past that they know at some level is very different from what it is supposed to be.

In sum, when parents are emotionally numb or when they restrict their emotional experience, they cannot be empathic and responsive to their children. People whose parents were very inaccessible often describe them in language that demonstrates how unemotional they seemed: "My mother was stunned by solitude," "My father was silent, he never talked or showed emotion," "My mother was a shadow, my father kept busy," "My mother seemed to be behind a pane of glass."[4] One man said, "You know, I don't know my parents. I'm thirty years old and I don't know my parents. They're like strangers to me."[5]

Janet Surrey emphasizes that the need to understand is as powerful as the need to be understood if engagement in relationship is to occur.[6] We have seen how hard it can be for children to have a sense of their parents when they are emotionally inaccessible and how much this loss contributes to the children's lack of a sense of their own truths and the validity of their own feelings. When parents are unaware of their own emotional experience, or have split off essential memories of the past, or are too preoccupied with just surviving psychologically, their children are left with a deep sense of shame about their own feelings. Consequently, they do not feel entitled to their own experience and are unable to be aware of and acknowledge their yearnings to know more about their parents — and about who they themselves really are.

H. Auerbach and E. Prelinger's detailed analysis of the treatment of a woman whose mother was a Holocaust survivor illustrates how knowing about this history gave some meaning to the lives of both the living and those who died. This woman recalled how hard she tried, as a child, to preserve her relationship with her inaccessible mother by struggling to understand her; she hoped that her mother could be more responsive to her if only she could be less preoccupied with the dead, about whom she rarely spoke. Despite how devastating the communications about the past were, the healing began in the treatment when the mother's behavior became more comprehensible to the daughter.[7]

Parentification

In some families children take on parental responsibility prematurely, at least in certain significant areas of family functioning. This is particularly true when an alcoholic or seriously depressed parent is involved. We use the term "parentification" to describe those family relationships in which parents expect and often demand that a child take on roles or perform them at a level inappropriate to the child's level of emotional, intellectual, and physical development.

The lack of mutuality between parent and child in these settings is evident when parents cannot reciprocate or be responsive to their children's needs; it is especially striking when parents cannot convey to their children a recognition of their efforts and contributions. One woman remembers, when she was around seven years old, covering her alcoholic mother with a blanket after she had passed out in the living room — and that in the morning her mother was oblivious of what had happened the night before.

Children who are parentified take over major household tasks when their parents are not available, including preparing meals and feeding younger siblings, often at very early ages. Most importantly, in families in which this dynamic occurs, the burden of responsibility that children assume for the well-being of others overrides their own entitlement to receive care and devotion, yet taking on this burden may be the only way they can make some connection with family members.

We know there are many cultural variations in what is expected of children. We see children's contributions to a family as very valuable and appropriate *if* the parents are empathic, responsive, and caretaking too. In learning how to listen and be responsive to their parents, children develop the capacity to empathize and to engage with others. However, when children must take care of parents long before they are cognitively and emotionally capable of handling the burdens this imposes, this activity becomes destructive. This is especially so when the children experience significant confusion or feelings of inadequacy in trying to respond to complex emotional situations which they can't possibly understand.

Nonmutual parentification often leads children growing up in these families to learn very early on to shut off their own needs and to have little expectation that others will want to know what these needs are. Despite their yearnings for connection, these children grow into adulthood regarding relationships in general as burdensome, nongratifying, and often incomprehensible. In their interactions they often continue to "take care" of others but with little access to their own feelings for other people.

In an interaction like the one we saw between Ann and Beth, their mutual engagement was a way of taking care of each other and it resulted in major shifts in their experience, with very positive consequences for their relationships with each other and with their friend Emily. But when a child must take care of parents whose complex psychological problems the child cannot begin to understand, let alone solve, she or he is left feeling unworthy, confused, depleted, and with a sense of hopelessness that anything can change.

In cases of divorce, when a mother often feels very alone and disconnected herself, she may increasingly turn to her children, often to a daughter, for help in managing the household. Some of these mothers tell of how they became depressed and relinquished many of the household responsibilities to their children. Many may have no choice but to turn to their children to assume more responsibility, especially when they have to work outside the home to support the family. But it is important to distinguish between mutual respect and mutual engagement in families where everyone pulls together to meet the new situation, on the one hand, and families where children are expected to assume a level of caretaking beyond their years and without reciprocity between parent and child, on the other.

The various modes of parentification we've described evolve out of the parents' demands and needs, without awareness and acknowledgment of the children's needs and level of development. As a consequence, relationships between these parents and their children are nonmutual. The child "takes care of" the parent not out of a growing mutual empathy and loving feelings, but out of fear of the parent's anger and out of the yearning to have some connection with that parent and not feel so disconnected and alone.

In addition, these situations force children to develop skills before they are truly ready developmentally to execute them with ease and a sense of mastery; instead, they will find the caretaking tasks difficult to perform and, consequently, will feel inadequate. These children end up sensing a great dissonance between how they are perceived by others and how they experience themselves.

The example of Carmen powerfully illustrates this pattern. Carmen entered therapy because she was very dissatisfied at work and could not imagine leaving her present job or looking for a new one. She had worked in the same company for many years but had never felt sufficiently recognized or appreciated. In the course of therapy it became clear that Carmen had a very low opinion of herself and that despite her complaints about her bosses, she believed she did not deserve their respect. She continually undervalued her skills, and when she did accomplish something important she would insist that "any *child* could do that."

Over time, as Carmen's family history unfolded, she realized how much she had been expected to do in her family. Her father died when she was nine, and her mother took over the family business. Carmen was expected to come to the office after school and to take on responsibilities beyond her years; she was always in a state of anxiety lest she disappoint her mother, who was often irritable and critical of her performance. Carmen was amazed to realize that this same state of anxiety was still with her in her current experience, but even more striking was her awareness that in the face of any new request made of her at work she would experience the same acute panic reaction she remembered as a child.

In such families the parents often fail to acknowledge the care and devotion that children give. Rather, they often criticize the child for not meeting their expectations. As a result, the child comes to believe that s/he is unworthy of trust and doesn't deserve a rightful place in the family. Under these circumstances, children often continue to try to please, to achieve, to take care of others, without any sense of the legitimacy of their own needs. They feel increasingly isolated, with little energy to engage with others in ways that can lead to greater self-awareness and self-worth. The capacity to establish authentic relationships with others under these circumstances diminishes. The appearance of connection belies the degree to which children growing up in such situations continue to stay out of connection.

CHRONIC DISCONNECTIONS

These common patterns — secrecy, inaccessibility of parents, and parentification of children — emerge from nonmutual family relationships and lead to chronic disconnections in the children growing up in these settings. These disconnections, in turn, lead to psychological problems, since they impede the development of mutually empathic relationships. To make matters worse, the parents in such families often offer little permission or opportunity for their children to seek help from, and connection with, others outside the family.

Children growing up in such households experience considerable pressure to stay in the family and not move out into the world. Parents are often very fearful of the dangers outside the family, in a world that seems to them hostile and dangerous, and are often isolated themselves. They experience very little mutuality in their relationships with their partners (if they have a partner) and look to their children as providers of the only relationships possible. But, as we have seen, they typically do not turn to their children through mutual engagement. Rather they wish, even if not always consciously, that their children will take over tasks they feel unable to manage themselves. Further, the need to hide family difficulties from "outsiders" contributes to keeping the children close to home, so that they will not divulge family secrets.

In such a context, children learn to doubt their inclinations to find other relational opportunities, feel there must be something bad about themselves if they resist their parents' demands for care-taking, and begin very early to alter themselves to fit what they see their parents expect of them. These children then feel disempow-ered, afraid that they will be unable to function outside the family because of their own profound self-doubt and shame and the need to maintain family secrets.

Even when children are neglected, when parents are unaware or unconcerned about where their children are, what they are doing, and how self-destructive or disturbed they are, families like these often maintain a facade of togetherness and a resistance to any in-fluence or interactions with people outside the family.

Some children try to resolve these issues by leaving home early, either by running away or by marrying young. They attempt to make a drastic, premature break, although their emotional invest-ments, worries, and preoccupations often remain with their original family, leaving little energy to engage in the new relationships they try to establish with others. They find ways to hide their vulnerabil-ities and tend to placate the people in their new relationships, be-cause they fear that otherwise they will be assaulted, terrorized, criticized, humiliated, and shamed.

Clearly, the psychological problems that result from families in which there are secrets, in which parents are relatively inaccessible, or in which children are parentified will vary along a continuum. Some people will grow into adults with more resilience than others; children from the same family may develop very differently.

Interestingly, recent research findings strongly suggest that the major factors contributing to resilience in children growing up in families characterized by extreme poverty, marital discord, deser-tion, divorce, and parental alcoholism and mental illness have to do with the importance of relationships.[8] For example, one major study reported that in addition to "temperamental" differences among children, evidence of a close relationship with at least one person and fewer prolonged separations from the primary caregiver during the first years of life operated as strong predictors of resilience in the children, even thirty years later. In fact, what the authors called temperamental variables are relational in nature. That is, the "resilient" children had the kind of temperaments that helped them with relationships from early in life. While very young they elicited positive attention from family members, nursery school teachers, social workers; the girls were described as "affectionate" and "cuddly," and the boys were described as "good-natured."[9]

It is very important not to pathologize members of all families that are usually considered at high risk for the development of psychological problems. We know that many people who grow up in troubled families emerge with great resilience and strength of character — despite all obstacles to empathic development, they become highly sensitive, caring people. When people encounter a relationship in which another person or persons can resonate with important aspects of their experience, the hope for more positive relational opportunities begins to move them along a new pathway.

The notion that this can happen only at the earliest stages of development is not persuasive. Often people in adolescence (and later) will find this resonance in a teacher, a coach, a friend, and then truly begin to turn their lives around; in many situations, family members — siblings, aunts, uncles — can offer a child some sense of another kind of relationship, one characterized by respect, empathy, and encouragement.

In the next chapter we will further explore the consequences of chronic and sustained disconnections among family members, that is, what people try to do about them — and in particular, the specific ways by which they try to find connection by staying out of connection.

6

SEEKING CONNECTION
BY STAYING OUT OF
CONNECTION

———

"Our whole life was an illusion," said a woman whose parents were both alcoholics.

> We looked like the all-American family, we had an upper-middle-class income, we had people who came over to the house, they weren't friends but they looked like friends. I was on the swimming team, my sister was a cheerleader, but if anybody had taken the time to look at any of us, none of us had any intimate relationships or ever talked to anybody about how they felt. . . . We were chameleons, put us in a situation, give us five minutes to watch the players and we adapt. . . . We will always feel outside of it but we can present ourselves however we need to present ourselves in order to exist.[1]

Another woman who grew up in an alcoholic family said, "I was addicted to having a relationship where I was in control; I was addicted to having somebody but not being in a relationship." Then she added, "Those are two different things."[2]

Both of these statements express profound feelings of disconnection, which these two women experienced even while presenting themselves or behaving "as if" they were in relationship. These quotes demonstrate the central relational paradox. Both women were aware that they were unable to represent themselves authentically, though they maintained some semblance of connection in order "to exist."

These women describe relationships that are very different from the healthy relationships of connection and mutual growth. Circumstances like theirs lead children to begin to form internally restricted relational images like those described in Chapter 4 — images that will guide them in determining what *not* to expect in relationships, images of how they believe they need to behave and what feelings they can express in order to maintain some connection with those available.

SURVIVAL THROUGH DISCONNECTION

The methods people develop to stay out of relationship are strategies of survival — people use them in the hope of warding off further wounding or violation. These strategies, then, begin as the form through which psychological problems are expressed. In fact, they now will *become* the main problem. As soon as people create strategies for staying out of relationships, they are contributing to disconnections — even as they yearn for connection. But it is essential to keep in mind that these strategies originally emerge out of a person's desperate efforts to find some way to make or preserve connection.

We all struggle with the central relational paradox and we all develop strategies to stay out of connection to some degree. For example, schoolchildren usually experience their teachers as powerful figures, and especially when teachers appear intimidating and critical, children invent strategies of disconnection. Some use the strategy of silence, of "disappearing," and they become adept at not being seen. Others adopt the role of the very good student, trying to figure out and conform to just what the teacher wants to win his or her approval. Another common strategy is to "act up," which might allow a child to feel more powerful, to engage the teacher's attention, and to have some sense of being able to predict or control the teacher's critical reactions.

While some of these strategies may appear to be more adaptive than others, in each of these instances, the child cannot truly represent who she or he is and will feel cut off from the teacher and often from other children. These different strategies do help a child feel less vulnerable to being exposed, criticized, and humiliated, but they also prevent the possibility of real connection with others.

There are, of course, many ways not to participate authentically and mutually in relationships. For example, some people manage through overinvestment in work to maintain their distance from others; some talk so much that others cannot get a word in.

Although they are not always aware of the discrepancy between their wish for connection, on the one hand, and the ways they distance themselves from others, on the other, people in the midst of this conflict report that they often feel a generalized level of anxiety and unease without knowing why. Typically they have developed the construction that the source of their discomfort lies in them — that it is their fault. If asked, they might report that their interactions with others produce the very opposite of "the five good things": a lack of zest, low self-esteem, a sense of powerlessness, a lack of understanding of why things go wrong, and a turning away from connection. Some feel "crazy," isolated, and out of touch with those around them. This "feeling crazy" often refers to their confusion about what they are feeling when there is no adequate response to them from other people.

Gender differences are relevant here. Because of cultural expectations, women probably make greater efforts to have some kind of connection with other people than do men, often through placating and accommodating those whom they perceive as more powerful and controlling. Of course, being accommodating to another person may be an expression of genuine, empathic connection; but it is problematic when the behavior does not arise from feelings and desires within the woman herself.

Certainly there are instances of men accommodating and placating others as a way of staying in some connection with them, as many women do, and they too will then be unable to engage with the other person in an authentic and mutual fashion; usually this happens in the context of nonmutual relationships with their bosses, fathers, or other men who are experienced as powerful authorities. However, men's strategies for staying out of relation more often take the form of avoidance, compulsive activity at work, or overinvolvement in activities like sports, and they make fewer efforts to establish connections. This may be largely due to the fact that the culture tends to want women to "take care of relationships," and to the fact that many men may already have other people available to them, both at home and at work (wives, secretaries), who are attentive and responsive to them, so that they are not as driven as women to develop relational strategies.

STRATEGIES FOR
STAYING OUT OF RELATIONSHIP

The three broad categories for staying out of relationship that we will discuss here obviously do not cover all possibilities, and they may overlap. However, they will help to illustrate some of the specific results of secrecy, the emotional inaccessibility of parents, and the parentification of children. They are (1) emotional disengagement in various forms that range from non-attention, preoccupation, or withdrawal to dissociative states and the use of substances which numb feelings; (2) role-playing, a style of "performing," which can seem adaptive and appropriate, but does not allow for the person's authentic engagement; and (3) replication, a replaying of old interactions and family dynamics that precludes participation in the present.

Emotional Disengagement

Earlier we noted that when parents are relatively cut off from their own feelings they are also inaccessible to their children, who soon learn to limit their own emotional expressiveness out of confusion and despair when no one responds. Typically, these children later describe their parents as emotionally flat, depressed, and depleted, with very low tolerance for any emotional expression by others.

Outbursts of rage and episodes of violence are often especially terrifying in these families since they often occur out of context, in settings otherwise so lacking in emotional life. These out-of-context emotional eruptions have been described in many families where one or both parents are unable to acknowledge their frustrations and underlying rage. Often such parents are replaying the explosive outbursts of their own parents in their families of origin.

Joyce entered therapy after she lost her temper with her five-year-old daughter, Wendy. She had thrown Wendy across the room after Wendy had drawn designs with red crayon on the living room wall. Joyce reported this incident with great shame and anxiety. She was amazed that she had reacted in such a violent fashion since she was not even aware of feeling angry when she first saw the drawings on the wall. She also talked about her pride in her home and how important it was to teach children to be respectful of their surroundings. In fact, Joyce was most animated when she described how much care went into decorating each room or when she was talking about how she cooked everything "from scratch."

Joyce's parents were both Holocaust survivors. Her mother was the only one in her family who had survived; her father, who had succeeded in rescuing two of his siblings, had lost everyone else. Joyce knew very little about her parents' history and from a young age had learned that her mother did not like to be questioned about her past. While her father was more forthcoming at times, his stories were not about the Holocaust years; rather they portrayed both of his parents' earlier lives in a very idealized way.

Joyce saw her mother as the stable and consistent person in the household; her father was chronically depressed and either worked outdoors on their farm or spent many hours of the day sleeping. She described her mother as devoted to the family, taking care of her father, sewing all of her and her sister's clothes, and cooking wonderful meals. While she admired her mother for her talents, she also described her as silent and noncommunicative; when her mother was not engaged in one of her many household tasks, she would retreat to the kitchen, where she did countless crossword puzzles. As a youngster, when Joyce tried to tell her mother about her concerns at school with her teachers or peers, her mother would look blank and offer the same response to all difficulties, large and small — "Oh, it's nothing. You'll see. It will work out."

It was only after Joyce had been in therapy for close to a year that she began to recall that her mother also had a terrible temper, which would erupt rarely but powerfully. She remembered her confusion and terror after one of these episodes since she didn't understand what she or her sister had done to provoke such anger. After these outbursts, her mother would disappear into her bedroom and never allude to the episode again. Only as Joyce began to have some understanding of her mother's isolation in life and how much effort her mother had to make to ward off all her painful feelings, could she begin to address the reasons for her own underlying feelings of sadness, frustration, and anger, feelings she had never allowed herself to experience consciously.

Children growing up in homes where their parents are unable to acknowledge or express their feelings in the context of their relationships develop little tolerance for their own emotions. They learn not to attend to their inner experience, even to doubt its validity, since they are deprived of the kind of mutual interactions that enable one to learn about one's feelings. With even more serious consequences, these children may come to believe that all emotions are dangerous.

People come to understand the context in which emotions develop only as they participate in mutual engagement with others. The possibilities for misunderstanding the meanings of expressed emotions are compounded in families whose emotional life is constricted, unpredictable, or punctuated by striking outbursts, especially if these families keep a painful piece of reality secret from others. In such family contexts, children do not feel safe in showing how they feel — even to themselves — and they are left to try to bear their feelings in isolation. It is not surprising that their emotions go underground, are numbed, split off, or unacknowledged.

In the case of Amy, discussed in the previous chapter, her parents' need to keep secret the death of her brother a year before she was born had an enormous impact on her capacity to experience, "own," and acknowledge her feelings. Through observing her parents' apparent inability to tolerate their own sadness, she developed the relational image that it would be unbearable and destructive to other people if she expressed painful feelings. Thus she had great difficulty staying with her own sadness in the face of painful losses and disappointments in her own life. Whenever she felt close to tears she would immediately shut off her feelings, terrified that if she ever let the tears flow, they would never stop and she would have a "nervous breakdown."

We know that people often use alcohol to deny pain and numb feelings. Alcoholics often report how drinking enables them to adapt to social situations and to look friendly and happy despite their enormous self-doubt and inability to engage authentically with people. The apparent conviviality in barrooms or at parties with a high consumption of alcohol often belies underlying feelings of loneliness and isolation among the participants.

The "blackout" phenomenon, in which an alcoholic seems to be participating with others and actively engaged in conversation and yet has absolutely no memory of the experience moments later, can serve as a metaphor for disconnection; the use of alcohol or drugs presents the illusion of connection, while the person continues to be shut off from authentic feelings, unable to relate to another person.

A child growing up with an alcoholic parent often experiences considerable confusion in trying to reconcile the "happy-go-lucky" image the parent projects in social settings and his/her numbness and flatness of emotional expression around real-life events in interactions with the child. In these families, too, explosive emotional outbursts may erupt apparently out of context, and children often learn very early on to distrust all emotional expression and keep a tight lid on all of their feelings.

In cases of incest, the young child is overwhelmed by physical and emotional sensations too intense to be assimilated. Some women with a history of incest can identify the moment when they were abused and learned to psychologically "leave" the situation by focusing on a patch of wallpaper, a pattern in the ceiling. One woman spoke poignantly of how this kept her out of relationship with other people throughout her life: "I have total recall of the most intimate details of different rooms I've been in. I can't remember who I was talking to or what we were talking about, but I sure can tell you exactly what the windows looked like!"[3]

This experience is enormously complicated because in most cases the young girl needs desperately to hold on to whatever relationships she has, even the relationship with her abuser, yet at the same time, she needs to remove herself emotionally from any engagement with him, which is at once so stimulating and so threatening.

Women who have grown up in families in which incest occurs use a range of other strategies for staying out of relationship, including substance abuse, to numb their experiences. Compulsive eating is another frequent way of staying out of engagement. The terror of being viciously exploited in relationships, as they have been in the past, combined with the simultaneous need to have relationships, often results in a lack of authenticity and experiences of dissonance and disingenuousness. One woman reported, "My facial expressions didn't match what I said. I was always grinning. I might be down in the dumps, three feet depressed, but I kept smiling no matter what, so the outside world wouldn't know how much pain I was in, couldn't guess my secret. That way they wouldn't fuck me."[4]

Role-Playing

The term "role-playing" covers a range of behaviors that reflect efforts to please, control, or gain the attention of significant people. Role-playing may be more or less problematic according to how pervasive it is and how nonauthentic, disengaged, or nonmutual the behaviors are.

A very common form of role-playing occurs whenever a person longs for a connection with someone who is more powerful and intimidating. Under such circumstances a person may quickly learn to read what the other person expects of him/her and then adopts that behavior, plays that role, to win that person's approval.

The strategy of role-playing can begin very early. When children learn that they must hide their feelings or feel powerless to have a genuine impact on the important people in their lives, they soon come to disbelieve their inner experience and behave instead according to what they see as the expectations of others, or they learn how to "manage" or "control" others to gain some response from them. In many of the families we've described, playing a role can serve to maintain family secrets and the denial of the truth of family problems, and to sustain the family myth that everyone is fine.

As they move into adulthood, children who learn to role-play develop personas that may become so firmly entrenched that they preclude authenticity in relational encounters. Role-playing can give the illusion of connection and of the presence of a real person when, in fact, the person is basically absent, not truly in touch with herself (or himself) and intent on behaving according to others' expectations. Role-playing can thus become a way of distancing from others. One man who is also a therapist writes, "I learned about smiling before I was five. . . . They all would smile back but they would never see me at all. I could sit behind my smile and watch."[5]

Many women take on the role of caretaker as a result of societal pressures, but some men do also. Obviously, this can be the result of being parentified as a child, but people who were not obviously parentified can also adopt this role as a strategy of disconnection, and in either case it often becomes generalized to other relationships. To the extent that caretaking behavior does not arise from the loving feelings of true connection, it does not lead to feelings of zest, empowerment, or worthiness, since the way the person assumes the role involves attending to but not really connecting with the other person. It can be extremely painful to keep doing "good things," and maybe even being praised by some, but never feel really good inside.

Under these circumstances, people learn how to do caretaking tasks through playing a role, but their empathic sensibilities are often blocked — an indication of the nonrelational aspects of this kind of role-playing. For example, it is not uncommon to hear from adults who have been very parentified as children how resentful they feel about the caretaking that they do (many of these children become aware of the resentment only after they've been in therapy). A woman from an incestuous family, who seemed very attentive to her ill father, said, "I can't afford to feel anything for my father. I would rather just do what I have to do for him, like a robot, treat him like a thing, that's what he does to my mother and me."

There are, of course, other roles people learn to play out in the family — the extrovert, the trouble-maker, the clown. What is most relevant is not the particular role assumed, but rather the need to keep oneself in a constricted range of functioning in order to deal with nonmutuality and unpredictability in the family.

In maintaining stereotyped behaviors, a person can have the illusion of knowing what to do in any eventuality and can avoid any emotional investment. Thus, through adopting a role, people can feel they are protecting themselves from being caught off guard, terrorized, disappointed, or wounded. At the same time, their role-playing is an attempt to gain some sense of connection with other members of the family.

Replication

Replication is a strategy that takes the form of a compelling and unrelenting need to repeat, over and over, old traumatic interactions. The notion of replaying old conflicts is hardly new and owes its origin to Freud's concept of the repetition compulsion.[6] Freud believed human beings needed to recreate traumatic experiences, in part to maintain the repression of these experiences and in part as an attempt to "master" the trauma. He saw these repetitions as essentially self-destructive since they do not lead to gratification or resolution of the conflicts.

However, if we take into account the central relational paradox, namely, how much people yearn to stay connected with the important people in their lives and yet how much they fear the experience of disconnection when they do risk engaging with them, then this propensity to replay old conflicts can be understood in a different way. For example, these repetitions may also operate to keep those who grow up in troubled families locked in the relationships of the past — trying again and again to find a connection with the main people in their families of origin — and out of authentic relationships in their current lives.

The propensity to repeat old behaviors is, of course, not limited to people with major early trauma. All of us replay old dramas to some degree; we hold on to patterns of interactions that can be traced back in our histories.

An example of replication can be seen in the story of Linda, a waitress, who had a lover, Laura, who was an alcoholic. Laura would spend the evening making the rounds of several bars. Linda would roam the streets, trying to identify her lover's car in order to make sure that she did not drive home drunk. Both of Linda's parents, who were alcoholics, had died in an automobile accident when she was fifteen. She recalled the many nights she and her grandmother would stay up until they heard the parents come home and knew they were safe. While these vigils were terrifying to Linda because her grandmother would pace the floor and wring her hands, the grandmother never spoke her fears out loud and Linda's parents' alcoholism was never mentioned. All of this nighttime activity had not saved her parents, but Linda stayed in some sense of connection with them by replaying the old drama and seeking to protect her lover from a similar fate.

When people who grow up in troubled families begin to recognize their propensity to repeat the very patterns they think they most want to eliminate, they are often very confused and can't make sense out of this. Yet, in listening to them, it becomes apparent that these old patterns at least have the advantage of being familiar and "known," while new or different ways of reacting can seem fraught with new dangers. This can be terrifying to people who have known a great deal of unpredictability and chaos in the past. At the same time, people may hope, at some level, that if given the chance to return to the old relational patterns they will find the connection they so desperately wanted, that this time they will have a chance to do it differently. Typically, they deeply believe that it is always their fault when these ways of behaving result in the same hurts that they experienced when they were growing up.

A good example of how the strategy of replication can lead to serious problems is reported by David Treadway in his book *Before It's Too Late*.[7] A fourteen-year-old girl came to therapy because of a drinking problem. Both parents and her siblings were also alcoholics. She quickly seemed to establish a very positive relationship with her therapist, stopped drinking, and did much better in all areas of her life. Then, the night before a scheduled therapy appointment, she attempted suicide, which took her therapist completely by surprise. Her explanation was telling: she said she had become frightened that she did not have a family anymore and didn't belong anywhere.

We could speculate that she felt safer returning to old patterns that brought her back into some connection with her family and at the same time protected her from the "danger" of a new, more genuine connection with her therapist. That is, to develop a more genuine relationship with her therapist may have felt like too great a risk to take — she may have feared she might once again end up feeling deeply disappointed, exposed, and humiliated by her needs and vulnerability. As adults who grew up in homes like these replay their early relationships, they remain psychologically in the familiar setting of their families, and often they avoid any intimacy with any one else.

Worries about the well-being of an alcoholic parent frequently pursue the child even after he or she has grown up and leaves home and marries. Fear that some calamity will occur if they are not there to prevent it often keeps the children of alcoholics from truly engaging in current relationships with their spouses and children. A woman named Alice spoke in therapy about her constant preoccupation with her mother's drinking when she was growing up; when she was at school she worried about whether her mother would be out cold on the floor when she came home, whether her mother's careless smoking would start a fire. She said she felt deeply attached to her mother, but in therapy she became aware of how little she was really connected, how little she ever knew about her, and of how distant and unapproachable her mother was. In a similar way, Alice had become obsessed with her husband's drinking and her constant terror of what accidents might befall him when he was away from home. She was quite isolated from other relationships, and despite her intense involvement with her husband in her thoughts, she felt very alone and bereft in her daily life.

Some people coping with past histories of trauma represent the second and even third generation of victims of violence or abuse. Sometimes this is literally so, as, for example, when the father who abused his daughter becomes the grandfather who abuses his granddaughter. Sometimes a parent's history is communicated to the child in powerful ways, so that the child experiences that story as her own. In both instances the trauma history becomes evident in the ways children growing up in these families tend to replay not only their own past, but also the victimization of parental figures. This replay of another generation's painful experience represents the desperate search for some degree of connection with a parent.

Children of Holocaust survivors often attempt to replay their parents' traumatic experiences. They may have nightmares, often recurrent, in which they are fleeing Nazis or other dangerous, aggressive figures, looking for a place to hide and feeling helpless about reaching safety. One woman expressed puzzlement about the vivid and powerful nature of such nightmares since she did not recall her parents ever speaking about their terrors or experiences.

Although Holocaust survivors do not typically talk about the horrors of what happened to them, sometimes they will tell one particularly painful vignette that powerfully conveys to their children the true nature of their experience. One survivor told her daughter that when she first arrived in Auschwitz, she saw truckloads of children being dumped into a bonfire and consumed alive; upon seeing this sight she began to bang her head against a wall in an attempt to kill herself. She wondered, "For what purpose were these children created?"[8] This sense of meaninglessness about the horrors of the Holocaust haunted the daughter and she constantly replayed these feelings in various forms in her life. She had recurrent dreams of this unspeakable experience. Her therapist believed them to be her attempt to recreate the emotions that she could not experience *with* her mother; the daughter felt that if she ceased dreaming these dreams she would be deserting her mother.

The daughter's dreams represented an attempt to understand, connect with, and help her mother survive. Initially she was not aware of the meaning of her attempts to replicate her mother's history, but she knew that she experienced her mother's alienation, isolation, and depression as her own. In this way, replications represent a most poignant attempt to be with the important people in one's life when it has been impossible to truly be with them. The child, in search of all of the "five good things" that follow from authentic engagement in mutual relationships, chases an illusion of relationship. She remains disempowered, often without valid knowledge of herself and others, feeling totally unworthy and out of connection, often taking on her parents' terrors, depression, or isolation, all the while believing it is all her fault.

We have illustrated some of the more striking strategies people have developed to try to deal with the dilemma of finding a way to make connections when they also have serious reasons to fear connections. There are others. Staying out of connection leaves people suffering in many ways, disempowered, and out of touch with themselves as well as others. But people can learn to create more authentic connections with others and thereby with their own experience. There are many paths to more authentic connection. Therapy is one. In the following chapters we will consider how our view of the significance of connection in human development influences and changes the practice of psychotherapy.

PART THREE

PSYCHOTHERAPY

7

A RELATIONAL REFRAMING
OF PSYCHOTHERAPY

━━

Our emphasis on connections and disconnections has had a powerful impact on the way we do therapy, leading us to a reframing of
the central goals, processes, and structure of our practice. We've become convinced that therapy must focus on understanding the
sources of disconnection and finding the ways to move from disconnection to connection — connection that is mutually empowering.

We believe that therapy has to provide a new relational experience, that the quality of the therapist–patient relationship is vital to
the healing process.[1] If a person can begin to feel that this connection is safe and authentic, she will feel able to go on to explore more
of her experience and can come to understand her strategies for disconnection, her relational images and their meanings, and the life
experiences that led to the creation of all of these. As she is able to

bring this vital material into the relationship with the therapist, she becomes increasingly connected. The therapy becomes a growing cycle in which enlarging connection leads to enlarging understanding and enlarging understanding leads to enlarging connection. As a result of this enlarging connection with the therapist, the patient can find ways to create more authentic connections with other people. Thus, therapy should lead to a connection that is mutually empowering in itself and also to mutually empowering connections with others.

Indeed, we believe that the goal of therapy is *precisely* mutual empowerment, including the "five good things" that result from mutually empathic connections, as described in Chapter 3. These "good things" are the overall goals or the endpoints of therapy, but patient and therapist can create parts of them at many steps along the way. Of course, they don't happen at every moment in therapy, but we can keep working toward them. However, both therapist and patient have to struggle with the forces within them that stand in the way of mutual empathy and mutual empowerment. We all grapple with these forces. We all carry in us the central relational paradox. This is what patient and therapist face as they undertake their work together.

Most traditional approaches to therapy focus on increased independence, greater self-knowledge or insight, or a stronger sense of self as endpoints of therapy. In contrast, we see the greater capacity for engaging in mutually empathic and mutually empowering connections as the goal. Out of this increased connection, the person becomes a fuller, stronger person as she simultaneously becomes more connected to her experience. To see how this approach differs from other approaches, it is necessary to examine the processes that we see as key to psychotherapy. Since our work focuses on the experience of women, we'll use the pronoun "she" most often, but, again, we argue that the work itself is relevant to all people.

THE BASIC GUIDE IN THERAPY

We believe the first and most basic guide in therapy is that the therapist must attend to how connected or disconnected she and the patient are at all times. In general, this emphasis contrasts with the traditional ways of working in therapy.

For example, over the years when we have heard therapists discuss their patients or when we have read case reports written by clinicians who were describing a patient's psychological difficulties, we have noted that the focus is usually on specific diagnoses, the patient's childhood, and amenability to therapy. Depending on the particular theoretical orientation, the discussion of a patient might focus on what childhood stages had not been adequately resolved, on what deficits the patient has experienced as a function of inadequate parenting at various stages of development, or on the observation that the parents were too narcissistic to be able to build their child's self-esteem. The therapeutic work is then organized around helping the patient gain the necessary insight to change, or providing corrective experiences to make up for previous deficits, or helping her feel more valued and to develop more pride and confidence in herself.

In contrast, our focus on the significance of disconnections in relationships leads us to speak differently about the people we treat. We are making the bold statement that most of the problems that people bring into therapy are reflections of the central relational paradox. In our view, a wide range of symptoms, such as phobias, anxiety, depression, dissociative states, paranoid ideas, self-sabotaging behaviors, and other problems reflect ways of attempting to stay out of relationship and to hide deep yearnings for connections.

For example, people who are paranoid typically become intensely involved with their suspicions regarding others. Their fears of betrayal and of being harmed reflect indirectly their intense longing for other people's loyalty and commitment, yet their suspiciousness serves to distance them from others and to push other people away. People who have phobias are often very avoidant of others since they become anxious in certain circumstances (for example, away from home, or in a confined area), yet they need other people to help them go places they can't go by themselves, or to extricate them from frightening circumstances. Thus, in the process of avoiding contact and pushing people away, they long for others to come and rescue them from their plight.

Two rather different stories from clinical practice illustrate our shift in language and approach. (In describing therapy, we'll use "I" rather than "we" since in each of these situations only one of us was involved.)

A forty-year-old woman we'll call Clara entered therapy because of a significant depression that had developed when she moved back to her hometown. She had looked forward to being closer to her family. Instead, once settled, Clara was unable to get a job, isolated herself from friends and family, stayed in bed all day, and felt irritable, bleak, and without energy. She said that she dragged herself to therapy and could not muster much interest in the process. I had to actively resist being pulled into her depressive spiral and feelings of hopelessness when I was with her. I noticed, however, that whenever I had the opportunity to focus on her particular day-to-day experiences and could join her in some of her concrete disappointments, I could feel something *with* her. At those times Clara would perk up and become more responsive.

After a session in which I noted how much she minimized the power of significant events in her life, she entered the next session unusually cheerful and recalled that that morning at the bank, the teller had said, "You know, you have a very nice smile." That made her feel good "for some reason," she said. I then said, "It feels good to be seen, to be noticed. You feel less alone." I reminded her that in therapy she had come to recognize more and more how much she had felt unseen in her family and how little she had believed that her problems were "serious enough" to be noticed. Rather, she had blamed herself for being too demanding and had thought there was something wrong with her.

Clara said that at that moment a memory came to mind of "a minor event" in her childhood. The memory was of herself at five years of age, coming home from school when a man appeared, pulled his pants down, and said, "This is for you." She recalled being terrified, starting to run and falling down, clutching the grass under her. At that moment a teacher arrived and the man fled; the teacher called her mother and she went home. Her mother reacted to her distress saying, "But nothing happened. Why are you making such a fuss?" Clara told me this without emotion, as though she herself saw it as a nonevent since "nothing *really* happened." My response was authentic surprise at her minimization, and I said with feeling that the terrifying images she presented in her story helped me see that something indeed *had* happened and that it must have had a powerful impact on her.

She then began to talk with much more energy, citing the various ways in which throughout adolescence, and even in a more recent (disguised but clear) sexual encounter, she had been haunted by that memory. Yet she always felt foolish about "making a fuss," and was never sure whether she had correctly perceived a given situation as a sexual threat or not; typically, she blamed herself for "misunderstanding" a situation and being too self-conscious. I then said, "It's so hard to believe something happened when it's questioned, and then you begin to wonder what's real and what isn't." She began to weep, and I felt her sadness in a way I had not before. Before this moment, I had certainly been aware of Clara's sadness, and I'd felt empathic with her, largely as a result of my understanding all the reasons for her sadness; however, when she shifted into this more direct, open expression of her feelings, I was moved to a new level of emotional understanding of what it was like for her — that is, I was brought to feel we were in more connection. Clara became perceptibly more engaged with me and less depressed.

This experience of being moved by a patient's feelings, authentically and powerfully, requires the therapist to be open to experiencing her own emotions; in this process therapists can allow themselves to be moved and to convey this at some level to their patients. Many therapists have been trained to distance themselves from their strong feelings, as if through feeling with their patients they would lose their "objectivity," their "neutrality," and their capacity to function therapeutically. But we believe it is the very openness to her own feelings that allows the therapist to truly resonate with patients as they begin, often for the first time, to be in touch with their feelings. And we do not believe that feelings keep therapists from good thinking and good judgment. Indeed, it is the reverse.

Clara's relational images became more apparent as she became less depressed and more connected in therapy. At one level she carried very idealized relational images of a family that was warm and caring and responsive. She believed that if only she could find ways to engage with the members of her family, by living near them and by being attentive to her parents, they would come through for her. Underneath these idealizations was another set of relational images that was less apparent to her and emerged later in the course of therapy. The latter reflected her deeper conviction that if she did express her longings for a loving and responsive family, these longings would never be attended to and she would not be able to have an impact on her parents and siblings. Instead, she would end up in despair because her belief that she was not worthy of their loving attention would be confirmed. Having two sets or levels of relational images is not uncommon; the more idealized one, which is more apparent on the surface, usually covers up a stronger conviction that longings for connection will be met with various degrees of disappointment and rejection.[2]

The central relational paradox was evident in the way Clara's depressive symptoms reflected her yearnings for connection while at the same time they kept her out of relationship with me and with her family. Her feelings of helplessness indirectly expressed her longings for connection, and her hopelessness showed her deep despair that she would never merit the kinds of connections she wanted from her family. That perspective pushed other people away and worked to keep Clara isolated.

In the session described above, when Clara did get in touch with her sadness and began to weep, she also began to move forward. She spoke of how her longings for closeness with her family had gone unfulfilled, and of how she often felt shut out by their lack of response to her. She saw how much she had isolated herself and retreated from *all* opportunities for connections as a consequence.

Pat, who was divorced and in her fifties, was an extremely energetic and accomplished woman. Her internist had suggested she seek therapy because of a weight gain of over seventy pounds in one year. At our initial interview she described how a lifetime of binge eating had gone out of control. She was also having difficulty sleeping. Her daughter's alcoholism had intensified over the past few years; she was becoming more angry and estranged from Pat. A son had recently become depressed; he had made a serious suicide attempt and refused to see his mother. Although Pat appeared very friendly and outgoing, and reported events with color and flare, I sometimes felt quite removed from her. Though I soon learned how much pain she felt, I was often not in touch with it in a way that helped me feel present and involved.

One day, Pat come in to a session saying she would like to ask a favor of me: "I want to just talk and I'd like you not to say anything until I'm finished." She then reported in detail a series of events involving different family members, all of which required her sacrificing her time, energy, and abilities in order to do things for them. I was not feeling very empathic; instead I felt critical of her doing so much for her family, who were not very appreciative as she portrayed them. Feeling more and more disconnected from her, I became increasingly bored, and as the hour progressed, it required enormous energy to keep awake. About forty minutes into the session, as she was coming to the end, I suddenly began to feel both very sad and wide awake. Pat had been saying, "I cried all last night." I was not completely clear about what happened, but I assume that as she had gradually become more open I had resonated with her ability to feel "something" about her underlying distress. As with Clara, I "felt" her sadness for the first time, and I became more present and authentic in response to something in her.

"We have to stop shortly," I said. "But I have to tell you something. I had a hard time today feeling in touch with you. I thought it was because you were protecting yourself in some way. There seemed to be a wall between us. I wonder if it is just that very feeling that you wanted to communicate to me, because you were feeling walled off from your own feelings and wanted me to know. I also understand that there are powerful reasons for you to feel terrible, but I couldn't really feel them with you . . . then suddenly I felt your sadness and heartbreak." Pat nodded, and said soberly, "I do feel terrible. I don't know what I'm going to do." She added, with much more feeling than ever before, "It feels hopeless to me." As we moved to the door I said, "The fact that you were able to feel that here, and I could feel it with you, tells me we're moving and I am really hopeful about that."

Pat's stories about what she had done for various family members, although hard to listen to, nevertheless did reveal the content of a set of her relational images and how they kept her out of connection. These images reflected her belief that only if she sacrificed her own needs and was continually attentive to others could she gain some sense of connection with them. I knew from Pat's history that she had started very early "taking care of" her parents and her siblings, so parentification was likely an issue. I believe that telling me these stories was her way of convincing me that she was a good person, yet in the process, she disconnected and distanced herself from me since she "took over" most of the session and left me out. I believe she was aware of both my growing distance from her and my efforts to be attentive. In her life she was probably continually disappointed when others were not grateful for all that she did for them. She could not see that her attentiveness to others may not have been expressed in a caring and authentic manner, that her relatives may have felt she was rather judgmental of them, often controlling, and not available emotionally. Yet the meanings of her underlying relational images were similar to Clara's in that she believed that she was really a bad person, unworthy of others' interest and attention.

Pat's strategies of survival all reflect the central relational paradox: they express both her yearnings for connection and her methods of staying out of relationship. Her food bingeing seemed to give her some sense of comfort and solace, yet it isolated her from others, since it was always done when she was alone and unobserved. Her desire to talk without comment from me reflected some attempt to engage me to listen to her, yet she did not truly let me in on how she was feeling, and I felt disconnected from her. Her sacrificing for other people allowed her to "take care" of them — and may have been an indirect expression of her own need to be taken care of — but it kept her out of authentic relationship.

As the therapy continued, Pat was able to talk about how alone she was in the world, how very painful it was to be so shut out by her children, and how much she longed for a closer relationship with them. Together we could acknowledge the value of her highly developed capacities to be responsive to others' needs and wishes, but that these qualities could only help her stay in authentic relationship if in the process she could also acknowledge her own vulnerabilities and her own yearnings. Pat felt more present and real to me as the two of us were able to engage more during our sessions. I did not feel boredom or sleepiness again, although we both continued to feel disconnected at times.

With both Clara and Pat, the whole relational dynamic began to shift as I struggled to move from an experience of disconnection to a greater sense of connection. As this shift occurred, each of these women felt more energetic and became gradually more empowered to risk exposing her vulnerability and to acknowledge at various levels her underlying wish for connection.

COMPONENTS OF A NEW RELATIONAL CONTEXT

Our focus on connections and disconnections as the basic issues in therapy leads us to emphasize certain significant components of the process. First, it is important to say that what we are always seeking in therapy is a particular kind of *movement,* one which combines two related senses of the word "move." As illustrated in the stories of Clara and Pat, we think change occurs when the therapist can feel *with* a person, that is, when the therapist can be moved emotionally by the person and the person can be moved by the therapist.

When the therapist can truly "be with" a patient's experience, something happens *in the therapist.* She is changed. If the patient can feel this happening, feel the therapist move in this sense, something very important occurs: she knows she has had an impact on the therapist simply by expressing her feelings and thoughts. This may be very new, and even hard to believe, but if a patient can begin to believe it, she will be moved in turn.

When this happens, it is because the patient has seen her impact on the therapist. Obviously, then, she is moving toward being empathic with the therapist. This is the essence of movement toward mutual empathy in the context of therapy — an experience that can begin the process by which the patient can move out of psychological isolation and the sense that she is alone with her fears or terrors. She begins to believe that another person can be with her in her important thoughts and feelings — she finds precisely the opposite of her worst fear.

Therapist and patient are in this movement together — they are both *moving in relationship*. The therapist too has the experience of being opened up; both are mutually engaged in the process. Each time such movement occurs, the patient mobilizes more of her empathic capacities. So does the therapist.

However, as the foregoing examples also illustrate, it is the therapist's responsibility to facilitate this movement. In the face of the power of the paradox, we believe that people can risk moving out of disconnection about their important experiences only if the therapist struggles to create an empathic and responsive relational context, not if the therapist is distant and affectively neutral.

Clara was able to begin to feel moved because I was so struck by her experience, especially by her having to feel it alone and then to have her feelings discounted. With Pat something shifted in her that led me to begin to feel her profound sadness. When I could truly feel that terrible sadness, we both became more able to "move in relationship."

To create this relational context, the therapist must make it very clear to the patient that she takes all of the patient's experience and emotions seriously. This may sound obvious, but we must remember that, like Clara and Pat, many people have been made to feel that their experience isn't important, doesn't matter. They will continue to feel this unless the therapist makes it very apparent through overt responses that she reacts differently from the people in the patient's past.

It follows that the therapist has to let the patient know when she has had an impact on the therapist. The therapist must make it palpable that this impact is moving her.

If, as with Clara and Pat, the therapist can keep working to create a relational context that includes the therapist's increasing authenticity and presence, an enlarging sense of connection will make it possible for the patient to start to move out of immobilization and hopelessness.

People often enter therapy believing that their feelings have no legitimacy and that no other person will ever be able to participate with them in their inner emotional life. In therapy they can change this belief. We believe that the work of therapy is to discover together how to find the paths toward movement in relationship. This means that the patient moves toward creating new relational images and meanings, meanings that can include more and more of the full and complex truth of her experience. She moves toward seeing the possibility that a relationship can include all of one's complicated mixture of feeling-thoughts, positive and negative, rational and irrational. She can feel and think about the feelings and sort them out in the process of experiencing them *with another person*. Experiencing them with another person is what she did not have the chance to do before.[3] We can probably talk about this best by citing another example.

A forty-year-old nurse we'll call Ellen came to therapy because of depression. She and her husband both held jobs; however, she took care of almost everything for their home life and their two children, eight and ten years old.

Initially, Ellen seemed to have relational images of herself as the "good daughter" and the "good wife" to her important parents and her important husband. She also had the image that others would allow her some connection only if she took care of all of their desires perfectly; it was her place to do that. These other people were important but she was not; her concerns were trivial and didn't matter.

I tried to convey empathy with almost everything Ellen talked about because I believed I felt it. For example, her husband often criticized her as if all the things she did for the family weren't enough. He expressed no recognition of the things she did do. When she took courses to increase her work skills, he belittled her efforts with jokes and put-downs.

I spoke of how hard it must be for her to feel she had no one with her in so many parts of her life. Ellen would reply in ways that tended to be self-derogatory — "But why do I let it bother me so much?" "Why do I need that? I'm not a child." I'd say something like "I think everyone needs that. It makes things feel good or bad in a basic way." This kind of work helped somewhat, but not enough.

The next step occurred after Ellen said again, "But why should I feel so bad about it?"

"Are you thinking that I should be able to make you feel better faster?" I asked.

"Oh, I'm certainly not criticizing you."

"I think you don't want to criticize me but you could have the wish that I would make you feel better faster."

"Well, sure I do."

There I made a guess from what I'd call "attempting to be empathic." I believed I could feel how much she didn't want to criticize me, but I could have been wrong. Maybe she did want to and I shouldn't have made it even harder. (This is the kind of choice that therapists cannot avoid. We can tell if we are wrong only by observing what happens next.) I thought, too, that she wished I'd just get her better. Traditionally, therapists can interpret such a wish in a number of ways. Ellen could be viewed as dependent or as seeing me as the omnipotent mother or in other such terms. However, I think such a wish is quite legitimate and I wanted to affirm that it was. I think we all have such wishes often. I said next something like "I'm guessing that you *so* want to feel better, and when we can't get there you could feel angry that *we* haven't made it happen. It's awful to feel awful." Ellen said, "Yes, but I know you're trying."

Again, there are a number of ways to hear this comment. For example, I could hear it as criticism — that is, I'm trying but I'm not doing so well. However, I felt that in this case Ellen was being empathic with me. I *was* trying and she knew that. I said, "Yes, I *am* trying. I know you feel that. It can be particularly hard to be dissatisfied or critical or angry if you also feel that I am trying."

At this point, the feelings really mounted. Ellen began to talk in a whole new way, very energized and with a great deal of sadness and anger. She said that no one ever cared how she felt or was interested in her, not in her own (original) family, not her husband. I was the first person who ever did. How could she want to hurt me? Yet she was discouraged with me and the therapy. She then talked of her deeply felt disappointment and anger at her own family. I was very moved and felt that she had advanced us to a new level of emotional and intellectual connection.

Ellen had contributed to this new connection in a major way and in a way that was particularly difficult for her, as it always is when one moves into previously forbidden or fearsome areas. She found that bringing into the relationship parts of her experience that she had not brought before led to more connection, not less. This step is the essence of growth. It may sound simple. It is not. It is the great discovery in therapy.

In addition, I felt affirmed because I felt that Ellen and I were both feeling something new in our interchange. Therapists feel enhanced as well when we feel we have had an impact.

Engaged in this way, Ellen now appeared a much stronger, more active woman. As we said about Ann and Beth, people feel enhanced and fulfilled when they can be actively engaged together about something that feels vital. Participating together in this way is very different from struggling alone without a sense of impact or response, or, alternatively, feeling that you have to hold back parts of yourself because you don't know "where the other person is" psychologically. This is what we mean by building increasing mutual empathy and mutual empowerment in therapy.

A more complete way to describe what happened is to say that the *relationship* between Ellen and me was enlarged and empowered. Together we now had more resources — more energy, action, knowledge, sense of worth, and sense of connection — in the relationship. These five components of any mutually empathic and mutually empowering connection were there for both of us.

It is not a question of giving or getting for one or the other, nor of being gratified or not gratified in the usual sense of those terms. Rather, at these moments of interchange, a person moves into more connection based on her more real representation of her experience. Simultaneously, she comes to feel in greater connection with her own inner experience, and to feel a *right* to that experience. She develops a more accurate awareness of herself as she becomes more accurately aware of the other person's responsiveness to her. She begins to create relational images in which the other person can be seen as more empathic and responsive. She, in turn, can be more truly and fully herself *and* simultaneously more truly with the other person.[4]

We have been struck, over the years, with how truly rare it is for women (and in other ways, men) in this culture to have a sense of a right to their own experience. (This is probably true in other cultures too, but we cannot speak for them.) The moments of finding and knowing one's own experience in therapy are, then, very profound and very moving for both patient and therapist.

From a larger point of view, not allowing women to acknowledge their own experience makes sense in the context of a patriarchally derived culture: women being able to know and speak their experience would profoundly disrupt the social structure. The consciousness-raising groups of the early part of the women's movement were built to counter this suppression of women's experience, and Carol Gilligan and her group have demonstrated the latter in girls who come up against "the wall of patriarchy" at adolescence and begin to "not know" about themselves and the world.[5] Intertwined with such general cultural influences, each nonmutually empowering family adds its own specific myths, as we discussed in Chapter 5, and each child in the family learns that she or he does not have the right to their experience if it disrupts these myths.

Judith Jordan's concept of "self-empathy" is pertinent here. She has written about how a person can develop empathy for her own experience — see it and understand it more fully and truthfully and compassionately. She can "feel with it" for what it has been and what has brought it about rather than in the critical and self-disparaging ways that she may have learned to feel about it. This empathy for our experience or for our past evolves out of engagement with another person(s) who is empathic about our experience — initially, more empathic than we ourselves can be. The empathy of others can lead us to more empathic understanding of ourselves.[6]

When people develop greater self-empathy, they usually have begun to change their relational images and their meanings. They've begun to believe that another person(s) can be empathic and responsive to them. They see other people and themselves in a new way.

These steps toward increased connection also contribute to the therapist's knowledge and ability to act in this particular relationship, and to her breadth and depth as a therapist and a person. Each patient will call for the therapist to stretch in certain dimensions and each therapy relationship will enlarge the therapist on several levels.[7]

Thus, the goal of therapy can be said to be increased connection — connection that is mutually empathic and mutually empowering. This is very different from dependency. Indeed, it is its opposite.

All therapists have talked about the therapeutic relationship. Very often in therapy, as in life, it is seen as a means to another end, such as individual development. We view it as both the means and the end. Judith Jordan has put it another way: "This relationship is the key to the process of therapy, not just the backdrop."[8]

Similarly, when we talk about the therapist stretching and enlarging, we mean that any mutually empathic and mutually empowering relationship is inevitably going to enlarge the therapist by virtue of the therapist participating in it. However, the purpose is *not* the therapist's enlargement, or, as it might be put in traditional literature, "the gratification of the therapist." The purpose is the patient's movement toward a more fulfilling life. The therapist's responsibility is always to work toward making it possible for the patient to bring more of her experience into the relationship and then to engage with the patient about *that* experience and *only* that experience.

As people come to believe that mutually empowering relationships are possible, they can begin to create new relational images. These images then allow them to alter their relationships in life outside of therapy, either by making efforts to change current relationships or by finding new and better ones. The therapist must work to make the therapeutic relationship empowering rather than dependent, so that therapy can be a time of transition from old, restricting relational images to new images of expanding possibilities.

Before moving into an exploration of therapy in greater depth and complexity, we will illustrate how this relational model requires a very different understanding and application of certain traditional concepts of therapy.

8

CHANGING TRADITIONAL
PSYCHOTHERAPY CONCEPTS

The concepts particularly relevant to our work are transference, countertransference, the unconscious, and resistance.

TRANSFERENCE

Freud originally developed the concept of transference when he noticed that his patients typically attributed to him, that is, "transferred" onto him, many of the feelings and perceptions they originally experienced with their parents and other important people in their lives. Thus, if a patient had experienced anger and resentment toward her father, she would unconsciously begin to feel similarly toward her therapist and to perceive her therapist as being "like her

father." Freud thought that through this process patients could re-
live their histories, with their therapists. The therapist's task would
then be to "interpret" how the patient had transferred feelings from
the past onto the therapist, and in this way help the patient gain an
understanding of the underlying reasons for his or her symptoms
and problems.

However, Freud believed that the transference could only develop if the therapist was very neutral and objective. He thought
that if the therapist revealed too much of his or her own personality,
the patient would not be able to "transfer" feelings from the past
onto the therapist in the present. According to Freud, the therapist
had to present a "blank screen" onto which the patient could easily
project unconscious feelings and thoughts from the past.

In our discussion of the reframing of transference and the ways
we use this phenomenon in the therapy relationship, we will focus
on two areas in which we differ from Freud's and other traditional
approaches: (1) we do not believe that the therapist needs to present
herself as neutral or as a "blank screen" in order for the transference
to emerge, and (2) we do not see interpreting the transference as the
major work of the therapy.

We believe that transference phenomena emerge in all relationships. That is, we all bring our experience with important relationships in the past into our current interactions with people — particularly through the relational images we carry with us. When we
discussed replication as a strategy of disconnection in Chapter 6, we
noted that all people to some extent replay old patterns of interaction, originally established in their families, in other important relationships in their lives. We said that replication becomes problematic when it keeps people "stuck in the past" and not free to engage
in new relationships in the present.

We believe that it is the very neutrality and distance of the traditional therapist that impede the way in which therapy can provide
a new and different experience. As long as the therapist remains
"neutral" or relatively noncommunicative, the patient may not perceive the significant *differences* between her relationship with the
therapist and those relational images from the past that she brings to
the therapy. For example, people who grew up in families with

emotionally inaccessible parents might perceive the "neutral" therapist as being as disconnecting as their parents were.[1]

In contrast, we believe that if the therapist is able to create a new relational context that is empathic and empowering, she will provide a more fertile ground for the essentials of transference to emerge. That is, the therapist will not prevent the transference from developing; instead, she will make it more possible. Moreover, it will occur in ways that the patient can more readily understand. We see transference as an avenue to learning some of the essentials of past relationships and to seeing how they impact the current therapy relationship. Memories of one's past relationships, with their history of connections and disconnections, shape the content and complexities of the relational images people bring into therapy. These images inform the expectations people have about relationships in general, but in therapy they become the focus of *exploration*. The therapist needs to be particularly attentive to how these images get "played out" in therapy, sometimes symbolically and without awareness, and often in displaced and distorted forms. Thus, contrary to the notion that it is the blank screen of the therapist that allows the transference to emerge, we believe that a genuine relational context provides the necessary *safety* and a conducive setting for both patient and therapist to become increasingly aware of the representations of these old relational images as they are expressed in the transference — and to begin to modify these old expectations about relationships.

A short vignette will best illustrate the power of the transference in an ongoing therapeutic relationship. As a result of a minor accident, I had a painful foot sprain and could walk only in running shoes. Jill, a woman I had been seeing for more than three years, entered the office the first day after my accident (she had seen me walk ahead of her with my running shoes and a decided limp) and began the session by commenting sarcastically, "So now in addition to everything else you do, you're out there running with your friends every morning." It was striking that Jill was so keenly aware of my shoes and yet appeared oblivious to my limp; ordinarily she was very sympathetic to any sign of discomfort on my part. Although this reaction appeared irrational, it made sense to me. I understood it as her expression of the kinds of feelings of inadequacy, envy, and anger that characterized her early relationship with her mother, who was very active and energetic, and expected her daughter to perform and achieve for her.

Following a more traditional approach, another therapist might have made the following interpretation to Jill: "You know, when I entered the office I was limping but you were unable to notice it because you had already developed a distorted picture of me, to fit with your image of your mother. You saw me as a demanding woman, like your mother, very active and energetic, and expecting you to be the same. You assumed, then, that I would be as critical of you as your mother was." The therapist might have offered other examples of Jill's "projections" of her mother's expectations in order to help Jill understand and give up these "distortions."

However, we are not at all persuaded that the therapist offering interpretations about the transference to the patient is necessarily as effective as we were taught it would be. These formulations can often be experienced as highly intellectualized, or as criticisms, and often they are not very meaningful to the patient. In this situation, I thought Jill would be humiliated to learn that she had "not seen" me limping into the office, and that she would have had difficulty accepting, or "believing," that her view of her mother so overpowered and distorted her perceptions and interactions in other relationships. I thought Jill might see me again as being like her "critical" mother.

In fact, I learned something about Jill's relationship with her mother at a deeper level as a result of this incident. Although I had been hearing her stories about her mother over the past three years, this was the first time I had really felt her anger and frustration — as she played these feelings out with me. I was moved in a new way by how painful it was for her to believe she always fell short of her mother's (and my) expectations and could never be "good enough." Instead of "interpreting" what happened in the transference, I felt this incident impelled me to become more empathic with the power of Jill's relational image ("I will always fall short of other

people's expectations of me"). I had a greater sense of how important it was to convey to her my respect for her style and her way of
authentically representing herself. I had a new sense of how awful
it felt to grow up with her demanding and critical mother, and I was
pleased to hear her anger emerging, even if indirectly. I tried harder
to convey my appreciation of her own qualities. While I did truly
admire them, I knew she didn't, caught as she was in defeating comparisons to her mother. Jill gradually became more cognizant of
how she often did "see" me as making the same demands on her that
her mother had. She then could more readily accept me as a person
in my own right and recognize that I did not have any investment
in her being the kind of person her mother admired.

In the relational model, as the two participants struggle to establish a sense of trust and mutuality, the therapist needs to be keenly
aware of the qualities the patient may project onto her as a function
of the transference, and of how much these qualities feel dissonant
with her own experience of herself; through the therapist's style of
engaging with the patient, she can then convey some of the significant differences between her relationship with the patient and those
disconnecting relationships in the past. For example, I thought it
would be very helpful for Jill to begin to see me as a person who had
different values and different ideas from her mother. In general, as
therapists, we try to create a new experience of relationship that will
differentiate us from the harmful relational images our patients
carry with them from the past.

Over time, Jill and I were able to gain greater clarity and under
standing about the kinds of relational images she carried with her.
She discovered that she always assumed that others would be disappointed in her because "I never accomplish anything important"
and that she thought other people would find her boring. We were
able to articulate one of her most prominent relational images: "No
one will want to engage with me because I am not energetic or accomplished enough." Together Jill and I explored how these expectations developed and she could begin to believe that I did not share
them. We began to find new ways of being in relationship. In the
process, she found herself drawn to people who were more conge-

nial with her style and did not expect her to be a person she was not. It was, however, very painful for Jill to come to terms with her recognition that her mother was disappointed in her and did not really approve of how she led her life.

COUNTERTRANSFERENCE

Countertransference refers to the therapist's conscious and unconscious feelings about the patient. These may be in part a response to the patient's transference reactions, and in part an expression of the personal issues that the therapist brings into the therapy relationship. For example, a therapist may develop very strong positive or negative feelings toward a patient because he or she reminds the therapist of her own son or daughter.

Over the years, the concept of countertransference has undergone more modification and elaboration than any other feature of therapy. Freud's notion was that countertransference feelings were an impediment to the process of therapy since the therapist had apparently not succeeded in being objective and neutral enough. Freud saw any feelings the therapist had toward the patient as suspect and as indications of the therapist's "unanalyzed neurotic conflicts." When therapists became aware of having "feelings for the patient" they were expected to return to their own analysts to "get rid of" these intrusions.[2]

In the 1950s, however, a new perspective emerged that moved away from this pathologizing view of countertransference to see it as an opportunity for the therapist to learn more about *the patient* through examining all the thoughts and feelings stirred up in the interaction.[3] Most therapists today acknowledge the use of countertransference as a positive force in the psychotherapy process since it offers a new understanding of the patient's experiences.[4] This experience can be very powerful.

For instance, therapists may begin to experience feelings for their patients or about themselves that seem uncomfortable and inconsistent with their conscious perspectives. They may wonder if they are unconsciously picking up feelings the patient is experiencing but cannot acknowledge and therefore may be communicating indirectly. If a therapist is aware of these dynamics, he or she can become more empathic and responsive to the patient's distress, as happened in the session with Clara described in Chapter 7.

These ideas are important contributions to a more "interactional" view of the process of psychotherapy, but even in this view the focus continues to be more on the issues the patient presents than on the mutuality of the therapeutic encounter.

Contrary to the original notion of therapist neutrality, we believe the therapist is always experiencing a wide range of thoughts and feelings at various levels of awareness and articulation. Therapists also bring their own complicated sets of relational images into any therapy relationship. Thus, in our view, countertransference includes all the factors that either facilitate or impede the therapist's ability to connect with a patient.[5]

Since we believe that movement and change happen through a focus on the connections and disconnections in the therapeutic relationship (both in the present — that is, the "here and now" of the ongoing relationship — and through the relational images from the past that inform the transference), countertransference becomes one of the central points of the therapeutic work. The therapist's careful attention to it provides the primary opportunity for enhancing mutuality in the therapeutic encounter.

The therapist's attentiveness to feeling disconnected *begins* the process of determining the sources of this feeling and communicating to the patient the thoughts and feelings that will help to move both therapist and patient back into connection.

We'll go back to a first-person account of working with Pat to illustrate this process in detail.

My countertransference with Pat involved an inability to feel her distress, and I felt alone and disconnected as a result. In the face of that disconnection I felt uncomfortable, removed from my own feelings, unable to be empathic, frustrated and at a loss. When I had little opportunity to interact for most of the hour, what helped me was this perspective on countertransference, observing my own feelings and using them to better understand hers.

Bored and fighting off my sleepiness, I was aware of a whole array of feelings. I was irritated with Pat's demonstrations of care-taking of relatives, putting her own needs aside in the process. I was also aware that Pat was trying to impress me with her "goodness" while pushing me away, disconnecting from me, at the same time. This awareness helped me make strenuous efforts to stay awake and pay attention to Pat and, especially, to realize how awful and disempowering it felt to be so shut out and disconnected. Feeling these dynamics, I then tried to interrupt this pattern.

I believe that my focus on the dynamics of the central relational paradox was communicated at some level, and did help Pat to tune in, even momentarily, to her own sadness, which, in turn, moved me. I had a sense of urgency to seize the moment of feeling "something," to move out of the awfulness of disconnection, and as a result I became less stuck and then more connected with Pat. In the course of this "movement in relationship," I could begin to communicate to Pat some aspects of what I had experienced in the session. I could begin to feel more authentic as I began the process of sharing how removed I felt, but I could do this only when I could identify some opening in Pat, that is, when I could begin to resonate with her pain.

I could then grasp the moment of feeling "something" and I became less stuck, but I don't think I would have shared my sense of being so removed with Pat if I hadn't sensed some opening up in her. For if we take seriously the paradox our patients bring into the therapy, of wanting connection but being too afraid to truly be in connection, we must honor their need to keep us at a distance. We can move toward connection only as we sense the possibility of moving together with the patient.

This leads to the extremely complicated question of "therapist's disclosure." This refers to how much the therapist shares and communicates of her own thoughts and feelings, which impede movement in the therapy and lead to disconnection. The therapist has to be exquisitely sensitive to how much a patient can "receive" the therapist's communication of boredom, anger, or other feelings that can be quite hurtful. As in the case of Pat, we do not have to go into detail about our inner reactions; our judgment about what to share with the patient needs to be guided primarily by what we believe will move the relationship, rather than what will relieve the therapist's discomfort, or allow the therapist to express herself. Indeed, we would rather talk about what will move the relationship toward mutuality than focus solely on disclosure.

Janet Surrey has suggested that nondisclosure may at times have as significant a consequence for the therapeutic process as would disclosure.[6] Sometimes the therapist's silence may have a very negative effect in working with patients who struggle with authenticity and vulnerability — they may interpret the therapist's lack of response as disapproval or as their own failure to relate well. Also, to "not tell" a patient some important reality about the therapist, which might have an impact on the therapy, might easily result in a serious disconnection in the treatment — for example, when the therapist's parent or child is very ill or dies. A major event of this nature may interfere with the therapist's ability to be fully present in the therapeutic relationship; the reason to tell the patient is not to make the therapist feel better *per se,* but to ensure that the therapist will be able to be more connected and that the patient not blame herself for the therapist's lack of emotional availability.

There can be, however, serious misunderstandings of the concept of mutuality, misunderstandings that have led some therapists to disclose more about their feelings and experiences than is necessarily helpful to their patients; indeed, some of these disclosures may be experienced by the patient as intrusive, burdensome, or sometimes overwhelming. For example, sometimes in the service of "being a good role model" for the patient, a therapist might tell a patient how he or she managed a particular event in the past, conveying to the patient that the patient should do the same. We see this instance of disclosure as particularly harmful since it intensifies the power inequities in the relationship, suggesting that the "therapist knows best," and it does not respect or encourage the patient's growing capacity to cope with that particular event in her own unique way. An extreme instance of the misuse of therapist disclosure and its impact on vulnerable patients can be seen when therapists who abuse their patients begin to disclose their own "problems" and discontent as a prelude to making sexual advances.

In fact, the question of disclosure is very complex. As soon as we move away from the traditional dictum of total nondisclosure, we have to make very careful judgments. Here is where therapists need good training, supervision, and ongoing discussions with peers.

All therapists have known the discomfort of feeling helpless in the face of a patient's dilemma and pain, of feeling afraid of being taken over by the intensity of some patients' experiences, of being fearful and angry as our strong feelings sometimes threaten to overwhelm us. We believe that it is through these experiences that therapists can know about their patients' feelings in a deeper way and also know themselves more profoundly. It is this deeper way of knowing that communicates to the patient that she has an impact on the therapist, and, as a consequence, that movement and change are possible.

THE UNCONSCIOUS

If the relational context develops so that the patient feels safer and safer over time and experiences the therapist as real, accessible, and truly participating in the therapeutic work, then memories do begin to emerge that were previously repressed, split off, or robbed of their meanings and importance. The notion that by presenting a correct interpretation with perfect timing, the therapist can lift the repression and cause the unconscious to become conscious and dramatic change to occur has not been part of our clinical experience — although it is a common movie scenario. Rather, we find that as the sense of connection between therapist and patient grows, the patient feels more understood and gains greater clarity in her feelings and thoughts. This clarity makes the patient more ready to understand the meanings of early experiences. It is in this process that the patient's old relational images become more articulated and the patient can begin to modify them in the context of a new and different relational experience with the therapist.

Another way to put this is to say that destructive relational experiences from a patient's past, which may have been too threatening even to look at before, can begin to emerge when the patient can trust that the therapist will be able to tolerate these experiences and will respond genuinely and effectively to them. As the patient feels more accepted, and can let go of old expectations arising from experiences in past relationships, she can bring more and more of her whole person into relationship with the therapist, thus gaining access to unconscious, or previously split-off, experiences.

RESISTANCE

Traditionally, the concept of resistance refers to the many ways patients were said to avoid, resist, and "defend against" becoming aware of painful memories and all the thoughts and feelings that they were afraid to acknowledge consciously. Particularly as they came closer to remembering an important event or to a greater awareness of underlying feelings, therapists said, patients would unconsciously resist the therapeutic process in many different ways, coming late to sessions, for example, or forgetting appointments, having "nothing to say," becoming angry and critical of the therapist, or neglecting to pay the bill.

Typically the concept of resistance has had the connotation of blaming the patient, and the therapist's task is to interpret the resistance and confront the patient with the various ways the resistance is played out.

In contrast, we see resistance as a method or methods of staying out of relationship. We find it helpful to think in terms of a person's fear of bringing parts of his or her experience into connection — while keeping in mind always that the person wants very much to make these connections. Rather than seeing resistance as a battle between therapist and patient, this approach helps the therapist to stay empathic with both sides of the central relational paradox, and thereby to legitimate for each person both the desire for connection and his or her reasons for fearing it. In our experience in therapy, we have found that this focus helps keep the flow of therapy moving from periods of disconnection to new and better connection. What has been called resistance is so basic to our concept of movement in therapy that we will elaborate on it further in the next chapter.

9

HONORING THE STRATEGIES
OF DISCONNECTION

———

THE FLOW OF THERAPY

Even the best possible relationships proceed through periods of connection to disconnection to reconnection. But reconnection is never merely going back to some good old place. When this process occurs, each person and the relationship itself inevitably move on to a new level, to being *more* than they were before. This growth to a new level may be a small step, and it does not go on at every minute of life or at the same rate for all people involved, but it happens at times for all of us. Children, especially, force adults to confront the need to grow. Their more original and sometimes urgent expressions of feelings and needs present us with the challenge of moving out of our old patterns if we are to engage with them as they put forward their experience.

We see therapy, too, as a process of moving repeatedly into disconnection then new connection. Indeed, one way to describe therapy is to say that it is a special place designed for working on disconnections (that's why it can be so hard) — and for learning to move on through the pain of disconnection to new connections (that's why it can be so fulfilling and enlarging for both people involved).

However, the movement into more connection itself leads to the most difficult parts of therapy because it threatens the person's strategies for disconnection. As the patient begins to shift away from the strategies she's developed for staying out of relationship she also moves further toward a greater sense of her longing for authentic connection; this longing, however, brings with it a sense of feeling very vulnerable. It is a very frightening place to be.

Why should this longing for more authentic connection in the therapy relationship create such fear and feelings of vulnerability? We know that women talk often about wanting relationships and wanting closeness with others. Yet in our culture women are taught to wall off important parts of themselves, and many women have come to believe that authentic expressions of who they are will not be acceptable or valued by the people they care about. To give up their old, constricted strategies or habits, which permit at least limited connection, in order to experience more authentic connection feels very risky.

EMPATHY WITH THE STRATEGIES OF DISCONNECTION

We want to emphasize our belief in the great importance of respecting these strategies of disconnection rather than viewing them as what therapists typically call defenses — something that the therapist hopes to get rid of as quickly as possible. Probably a patient's greatest fear in therapy is the fear of changing, of giving up those ways of feeling and acting that, although not really helpful, seemed to promise some power, some strength.

In other words, it can be terribly difficult to give up one's strategies for staying out of authentic connection because they are in some sense adaptive — that is, they arise when the only relationships that are available are in some fundamental way disconnecting or even destructive: at some point in a person's history there was good reason to develop these strategies.

Instead of labeling such behaviors in therapy as resistance, we think of them as lifesaving — or mind-saving — strategies that people have developed for a reason. Sometimes patients are saying, in effect, "No, I won't engage with you because that means I have to turn into what you want me to be, and if I did that I would lose myself." This stance most likely evolved as a survival maneuver. It is a strategy that makes it difficult to form a relationship in therapy, but it deserves the therapist's respect and attention.

The experience of disconnection often leads people to form relational images of others as people who cannot understand, cannot feel with them, will not be there for them, will leave them in isolation, will turn against them, will scorn, humiliate, or abuse them. Within these expectations they develop a variety of responses: for example, they believe they must be compliant or silent, serving and responding to others' needs, not asking anything or outwitting, controlling, or triumphing over others. They may have to respond to other people in all kinds of complicated ways, as we suggested in Chapters 5 and 6, but what they cannot do is respond with their own thoughts and feelings.

For example, a woman who had a very violent father described how she "shriveled up" and tried to avoid his noticing her as a child. She developed a strategy of making herself invisible in general. As she grew up, she felt more in control and more powerful the more totally she could hide. (Indeed, it was amazing how effectively she, a very competent woman, got herself ignored.)

As we discussed earlier, in their studies of adolescents, Carol Gilligan and her colleagues have illuminated how girls react to the destructive forms of relationship our culture imposes on them, by developing less direct ways of relating.[1] In the face of relationships that violate one's very being, there is great validity in their response: it represents what Gilligan calls resistance to the dominant patriarchal culture's imposition on them. We would call it a strategy of disconnection. Many women later find in therapy the valuable parts of themselves which they could not bring into the only kinds of connection that are offered to girls and women.

The history of a woman with multiple personalities dramatically illustrates the authenticity contained in these strategies. As a child, she had been brutally sexually abused. Her main personality was very likeable and compliant. One of the others was an adolescent boy who was very angry, threw things, and made life very difficult for all concerned. This personality carried the woman's anger and noncompliance. It was very important that the therapist and others involved in her treatment honor the importance of the oppositional part of this woman as the only expression so far available to her of the outrage she felt at the violation she had experienced.

Therapists must be empathic with patients' strategies for avoiding connection — whether they are extreme or subtle — and sensitive to their need for these strategies and the terror of being without them. (Sometimes therapy can become stuck because a therapist falls into thinking of these strategies as getting in the way of her agenda as a therapist and so cannot be fully empathic with the need for them or understand their complexities.)

For example, I thought that a patient I'll call Eve probably needed to recognize her grief about the loss of her mother, but she seemed unable to do so. Instead she ran around in a frenzy of activity. From what she had told me about her family, I felt that I understood a lot about Eve's being unable to bring her feelings of grief into connection, but it was only when Eve said that the prospect of anyone seeing her feeling sad made her feel like a totally ugly creature, like "some kind of slimy bug found crawling in the mud," that I saw how the act of revealing her sadness would have felt to her. In Eve's relational images, no one could tolerate her feelings of distress or sadness, and other people demanded that she always look cheerful, competent, and pretty — that is, on top of things. To appear otherwise meant to be a failure, a total mess physically and in all other ways.

I didn't see Eve in this way at all, and I had not been fully empathic with all of the implications of what sadness meant to her. I said something like "Now I can feel much more how awful it feels even to think of expressing sadness." But it was probably not what I said but the fact that I was moved by the image Eve painted that changed the feeling between us and helped her believe I could be with her if she chose to express her feelings more directly.

Thinking about strategies of staying out of connection in this way can make a big difference in our whole attitude and approach. We can feel a new kind of respect and honoring — even admiration — for some of the strategies patients have developed even as we believe these strategies are making problems for the patients themselves, and for the therapist. Most important, knowing how patients may "need" their strategies for avoiding connection can help us to stay empathic with this side of the relational paradox, that is, the very side that is militating toward staying out of connection.

In saying this, we want to emphasize that it is not just a question of an intellectual understanding of a patient's strategies. That is important, but the therapist must really be able to "get with" the feeling of them. This combination of thought and feeling makes the difference; it allows the patient to "feel the therapist feeling with her" so that the therapy *moves*.

This is important because these strategies are usually the parts of therapy that make the most trouble; they can be very frustrating for the therapist. They are the parts that make many people seem most off-putting or angry-making. They are the parts that lead therapists to put pejorative diagnostic labels on people, calling them narcissistic personalities, borderline personalities, and the like, or describing them as "manipulative," "entitled," "hysterical," and so on. This kind of labeling allows the therapist to stay out of connection and does the patient a great deal of harm.

Empathy for her strategies of disconnection adds to our understanding of Pat, the woman who asked me not to talk for a whole visit, whom we discussed in Chapter 7. I began to understand that Pat was feeling more connected to me. That was probably why she was trying so hard to convince me that she was such a worthwhile person; and it was precisely this change that required her to remobilize her strategies of distancing and disconnection. My recognition of this change helped me stay more connected with Pat, even when she pushed me away; I had to respect her continued need to keep me at a distance, especially at those moments when she felt more of her yearnings for connection.

RUTH

A description of a period in therapy with Ruth, a very accomplished young woman in her thirties, may help to further illustrate these points. Ruth came to therapy for several reasons. She was very competent in her work but had some problems there. She also had a number of physical symptoms. Her several affairs with women had usually ended with a gradual decrease in passion and an increase in irritability, leading to her lovers leaving her.

Ruth had a very clever, articulate, and witty way of talking, often using ridicule and contempt in speaking of the many people she criticized. I often felt put off and ineffectual and also critical of her contemptuous approach. This was particularly so when I felt this fire indirectly turned on me. Because I didn't believe it would be helpful to express criticism, I probably used a strategy for staying out of connection — which was to be more silent.

What helped me was that in the course of our work together, I learned that Ruth was probably replicating her father's style of relating to others. She described him as clever and she admired his sarcastic put-downs of others. However, this replication never really brought her into greater connection with him and it alienated her from other relationships. Ruth had initially described both parents as loving, sometimes doing fun things with the children. However, it was becoming apparent to Ruth that her father was probably a heavy drinker, which she had never recognized before. She remembered many occasions when her mother spent time with her, but it was becoming clearer that there were also important times when her mother was psychologically not there for her. She was beginning to realize that her mother was probably often depressed and preoccupied with attending to her father.

She talked a little about what it would have been like to raise questions in her family about her father's drinking and realized that it felt, even now, like an absolute impossibility. She said no one would tolerate hearing it and in fact would turn on her and attack her. She began to get the sense that she may have been caught up in the family's denial and secrecy about this whole topic.

As with Clara, whom we described in Chapter 7, Ruth seemed to have two sets of relational images. In one set, she had an idealized image of being with good parents who were with her and who enjoyed being with her. In the other, neither of them could tolerate Ruth speaking the truth of her experience. She could be in connection with them only if she behaved as if there were no problems in the family and that they were all happy together, that is, if she upheld the first set of relational images.

At this time, Ruth spoke of remembering a specific incident when she was ill and really wanted her mother, but her mother had been unresponsive. She spoke of being able to feel that longing and of feeling terribly alone, frightened, and humiliated to even think about feeling this desire and having it be rejected. From the way she spoke, it was clear that this was an important step. She talked haltingly, without any of her cleverness and wit. As she told of her longing, she spoke with much more fear. I was very moved and felt that we were really making progress.

At the next session, Ruth seemed totally back to her old clever style. She conveyed none of the emotion of the prior session. I felt pushed away and much less connected. But she did bring a dream. In the dream there was a terrible explosion in a house. Ruth knew that a child was in the house and she was struggling through it to reach the child. She had a sense that other people were there, too. She managed to reach the child, who was lying unconscious. Now, however, no one else was there.

As Ruth and I discussed the dream, we talked about the feeling that an emotional explosion would have occurred in her family if she had spoken of what was probably going on, and also about how she felt she would be badly hurt if she stated her experience and then there was no one there to be with her. Perhaps she had learned to become "unconscious" — to not know — of the troubles in the family. She herself, however, did search for the hurt child and did want to help her but then was left all alone; I raised the possibility that the dream might also portray her fear that I, too, would not be there with her when she needed me, when she was feeling hurt, alone, and bereft.

Ruth discussed all this, but without much feeling, and despite the important content, the session was quite dull by contrast with the very moving prior session. However, I felt that Ruth's creating and remembering the dream and then bringing it in conveyed the other side of the paradox and represented her attempt to stay connected. In addition, the explosion image in the dream taught both of us how terrifying it felt to move further into her feelings about her family's denial and into the recognition that her parents had not been responsive to her in important ways. Ruth was probably beginning to feel that I could be with her when she talked about these feelings. She just couldn't proceed without having a chance to recognize more fully how frightening it was and without making more certain that I knew that.

Within a short time Ruth returned to her growing recognition of the ways her parents hadn't been emotionally responsive to her. However, the pattern of following this moving connection with periods of clever, nonfeeling conversation was repeated many more times in various forms. At these times, I had to deal with the disappointment I felt when I thought that Ruth and I were moving forward and then found Ruth back to her old style. When this happened, I would feel immobilized and without impact, shut out and not connected. But both Ruth and I were able to keep finding the ways to a new connection.

However, I especially want to highlight the dream because it so well illustrates what we have called the relational paradox and also because it helped me to really "get with" Ruth's strategies for staying out of connection. It told about the reasons for retreating from connection, for continuing the strategies of disconnection, and at the same time, the dream itself was a way of moving toward connection. The images of the explosion and the hurt child helped me feel more deeply how terrifying it was to see and speak the truth of Ruth's experience in her family, and how painful is the feeling of being so hurt with no one there to respond. In a way, this is one of those dreams that is everywoman's — and everyman's — dream.

The dream helped both Ruth and me explore the two levels of relational images with which she was dealing. Part of her longed to maintain the image of the idealized parents, but her other relational images were becoming clearer. Not only did she believe that truthful statements of her thoughts and feelings could not be tolerated, she believed they would cause violent total destruction of the whole family. However, she seemed to glimpse a new possibility in the dream: she might survive and she might be able to pay attention to the hurt, wounded child. Perhaps she was now going to be able to do that, to attend to the truth of that child's experience rather than the mythic overlay that denied it.

An illustration of a therapeutic experience with added complexity can help us to further understand the issue of being empathic with strategies for disconnection.

SALLY

Sally came to see me after she had broken her leg in a skiing accident and become seriously depressed. I had first met her thirteen years earlier, when she was seventeen. At that time she had also been depressed, as well as guilty about "sleeping around." She had described herself as a very good student and a superb athlete. She was clearly very competent and proud of her independence. But although she was popular at school, she felt isolated and had no close friends.

I had learned very little about her family at that time, except that they were working-class people and very religious. I did know that her mother was an alcoholic and that Sally had taken over many of the household tasks while growing up. She rarely mentioned her father, whom she described as very rigid, controlling, and often angry. She was "hyper-independent" in that she would always insist on taking care of everything herself and showing how competent she was. She also said that her parents would be very disapproving if she asked for help. She believed her family would be horrified to learn of her sexual promiscuity because they were so proper and religious.

Although she was appealing and responsive, I had always felt uneasy about how little I really knew about how bad Sally was feeling. For example, on two occasions I had been surprised to learn that she was seriously considering suicide. In looking back, I see how much she stayed out of relationship through her pleasant social manner and her highly developed independence. We did a lot of work around her ability to better tolerate her need for others and to gain a greater acceptance of her sexuality. She did improve over a period of three years as she became less isolated and depressed. In college, she pursued a career in accounting and was an active member of the college tennis team. She was no longer sexually promiscuous and was able to establish a relationship with a young man. She was very much in love and happy when we agreed to end this first round of therapy.

When we met again, Sally was thirty years old and living with a man she had met three years earlier, but since her accident their relationship had become more problematic. The fracture had been severe and she had already undergone several surgeries and had been immobilized for some months. During this time she began to have flashbacks of sexual abuse; she recalled her father molesting her between the ages of six and nine. She remembered, too, that at age nine, when she finally told her mother about the abuse, her mother called her a liar, but her father did stop the abuse. Although she could convey the horror of these flashbacks, she was very disinclined to talk about them. Still, the very fact that she could tell me about them suggested that she was feeling more connected to me than in our first encounter, and I did feel more connected to her.

In contrast to the energetic, active woman I remembered from before, Sally now seemed passive and disengaged. In addition to her broken leg, she was preoccupied with somatic complaints — aches, pains, and a chronic cough. Although she seemed pleased to be seeing me again, she was having major interpersonal difficulties everywhere else in her life, especially with her orthopedist, her physical therapist, and the other physicians she was seeing.

She became increasingly isolated and I was the one person who she felt was on her side. I began to get calls from her doctors, who were frustrated and perplexed in their work with her. They all felt that once her leg was better she would be able to resume playing tennis and doing other activities, which were important outlets for her and had been very adaptive in the past. But it became increasingly apparent that Sally was deliberately sabotaging efforts to get better. She was using her leg prematurely, often stamping and pounding it, not doing the prescribed exercises, and the like. She cancelled physical therapy appointments and would get into struggles about methods of treatment. Sally claimed she was simply expressing her frustration about how long it was taking to get better and how incompetent her doctors were. She insisted that she was very eager to get well.

I believe that Sally was feeling increasingly connected to me and I was becoming the only person whom she felt she could count on. But this was also frightening to her, which may have intensified her sabotaging behavior. What seemed even more troublesome was her resistance to going back to work. She had been an outstanding member of the organization she worked for, and the company's good health benefits covered most of her medical and psychotherapy expenses. Since the accident, however, her performance had been declining; she often called in sick and her latest evaluation had indicated that her job might be at risk. Her depression worsened, which she attributed to how badly everyone was treating her. There was also a significant increase in her suicidal ideation, and even more disturbing was the fact that she was very uncommunicative about this.

I found myself becoming increasingly frustrated, fearful that Sally would hurt herself and jeopardize her own physical and psychological recovery, her job, and all the benefits that were crucial to the continuation of her treatment. As I began to join her boyfriend and doctors in urging her to show up for work and to attend to her leg, she became more angry and difficult with me as well. I felt more and more helpless, angry, and fearful myself. Then she began to distance from me as she intensified her strategies, which moved both of us from connection to disconnection.

My understanding at that time was that Sally was playing out old relational images. Because she believed no one would be responsive to her yearnings for connection, they were expressed with hostility, which pushed people away and thus confirmed her expectations and fears that no one would be responsive to her. This is the kind of pattern that keeps old relational images entrenched and so difficult to modify. Both sides of the paradox were illustrated by her yearnings for connection, expressed through sabotaging the healing of her leg, on the one hand, which kept her in a "dependent" position with me and all her other treaters, and by her strategies to keep others at a distance through her angry demands, on the other.

In the language of more traditional approaches, one might say that Sally was "regressing" to a more dependent and childlike position and that her therapist and other treaters had to be careful not to encourage this regression; instead they needed to help her to become "more responsible." It became increasingly apparent, however, that the more Sally was urged to become more "responsible," the more she dug her heels in and would not move.

One day she said to me that she'd been surprised to hear herself tell her boyfriend, "I really don't think I want to work anymore." She then added, quite gleefully, "Boy, you should have seen the look on his face." At that moment my whole understanding shifted. It was the first time she *spoke*, rather than acted out, her wish to give in to her longing to be taken care of, not to have to work so hard.

Although the statement to her boyfriend was provocative in the same way as her actings out had been, it was an authentic expression of Sally's wish to give up all those strategies she had used to gain approval while staying out of authentic connection — including her competence at her job. As I began to see more of what it had been like for her and to resonate with her deep yearnings for the care she had never had, I could begin to empathize more fully with the enormous dilemma she faced. It was terrifying for her to acknowledge her yearnings more openly, since her old relational images informed her that she could not expect that others could respond to them and, indeed, would abuse her if she allowed herself to be vulnerable. I was then able to give up gradually my own strategies of distancing, which were largely a function of my fear that I would not be able to help her.

I felt much more connected with Sally as I developed a sense of how hard she had always tried to be sensible and competent, and how alone and unrecognized she felt. Something shifted in my capacity to be truly moved by her and to convey that back to her. Later, I was able to come back to my sense of her gleefulness in describing her boyfriend's reaction. I told her that I guessed it gave her some pleasure to say out loud what she may have wanted to say for some time; namely, that she sometimes got tired of working so hard. I said that it made me feel more hopeful whenever she was able to risk expressing her true feelings and thoughts. She began to talk with much more emotion about how scared she had been since she'd broken her leg, scared that she couldn't be in control anymore, and about how terrified she was that no one would put up with her, help her when she needed them. She began to see that she had developed these relational images very early, when there was either no response or a violating one to the expression of her painful feelings and thoughts. These images dominated her without her having any clear awareness of the assumptions and expectations she carried with her into all relationships. And her survival strategies continued to distance her from others.

My empathy with Sally's desperate need for her off-putting strategies, and with her terror of giving them up, helped me tolerate her more difficult behaviors. In time, Sally herself was able to see how much she was jeopardizing her own welfare by her strategies of disconnection in the face of her longing for connection. Over time, in a context of increased trust, we could proceed to address the powerful impact of her abuse history.

FROM DISCONNECTIONS TO CONNECTIONS

The cases of Ruth and Sally illustrate our perspective on different material, yet the therapeutic attitudes, issues, and processes involved are similar.

Ruth carried one set of relational images portraying an idealized family, which served as a kind of survival myth to guard against the pain of acknowledging certain truths about her actual family. To acknowledge those truths would only have alienated her from family members whom she still needed to be present in her life; but *not* to acknowledge them kept a large part of herself out of all of her relationships.

As Ruth began to see her family more realistically, she too articulated a deeper level of sets of relational images, namely that it was dangerous to speak the truth, to represent the reality of her experience in her family. As I, in turn, began to get a better sense of the truth of Ruth's experience, I began to feel very moved by Ruth's disappointments and fears. Ruth's movement and change then became more evident. My empathy with Ruth's fear of giving up her strategies also helped me stay connected whenever Ruth withdrew from me again.

It is often at these junctures, where a person begins to move toward connection and then needs to return to old strategies, that therapists tend to become discouraged, feel pushed out, and mobilize their own strategies of staying out of relationship, all without full consciousness — a pattern that may lead to further disconnection. In this instance, through empathy I was able to feel with Ruth's need to return to her old strategies. As a result, Ruth was able to be more in touch with the truth of her experience, which made it possible for her to create her dream and bring it into therapy. Visual images, such as those in dreams or those sometimes evoked as a person brings telling vignettes into the therapy hour (the hurt child in Ruth's dream or Eve's self-image as a slimy bug), often have a much more powerful emotional impact on the therapist than do verbal communications.

After Sally broke her leg, her strategies of exaggerated independence and an action mode failed her for the first time. For years she had avoided awareness of her yearnings for connection since she was so afraid that if she did need anyone she would be hurt or abused. Now, injured, and without recourse to her old strategies, she was forced to face her need for others and her longings for connection. Such longings were so terrifying that she then had to mobilize new strategies of disconnection. Since at a deep level she carried the assumption that no one would respond or attend to her unless coerced to do so, she felt she had to resort to controlling and forcing others to do what she wanted. These techniques, however, served to antagonize the very people she most needed. These are characteristic strategies of those people who are often called "help-rejecting" — people who feel helpless but are afraid to reveal their need for others, thus their very demands for help are expressed in an angry and aggressive fashion. These techniques provide an illusion of being in control and getting what one wants, but they serve only to intensify feelings of disconnection and alienation.

Sally's angry and demanding style alienated those to whom she most wanted to turn, but these behaviors also expressed her authentic resistance to accommodating to others, her rage at how people had let her down and violated her in the past, and her powerful wish to stop working so hard at being so sensible and independent.

At first, failing to be with her, I tried to persuade Sally that everyone wanted to be helpful to her. Further, I became caught up in trying to help her see that she was jeopardizing her health and her job. I could not keep in touch with how terrified she was of relinquishing her strategies, which would leave her feeling powerless and out of control. My own strategies of distancing were then called into play, as I assumed the role of the expert who would tell her what to do. My frustration and my sense of urgency to get her to change her behavior only made matters worse and I became increasingly distanced from her. At some level I think I wanted a return of the old hyper-independent Sally, who took care of herself and was so reasonable and accommodating. I was not very comfortable with this angry, rebellious person who frustrated all my good intentions to help her get better.

It was only when Sally told me indirectly that she did not want to work anymore, in a way which felt like a momentary revelation combined with an odd emotion of gleefulness, that something powerful shifted in me. These are the big moments in therapy, those "turning points" when the patient makes a new step in representing her (or his) experience more truthfully and the therapist "catches on" and tunes in to the underlying feelings. At that moment, I was very moved by a new emotional awareness of how burdened Sally had felt all her life, working so hard to do what others expected while always keeping herself aloof and out of relationship. She had never dared to express how fearful and helpless she felt, how she longed to be able to turn to others for some sense of authentic connection.

As I was able to identify the legitimacy of these feelings, to stay in tune with her terror at her sense of helplessness, Sally became more present and I felt less disconnected from her. As in my experience with Ruth, the patterns of moving in and out of connection as we worked on these issues became very evident. Sally would become more suicidal, and more difficult to engage, after a more genuine encounter, but as I began to appreciate and empathize with this process, we could continue to move back into connection — again and again. Later she she could tell me that the experience of being heard and seen in her pain and terror had allowed her to begin to hope that she did not have to be so alone in her life. But, as we have emphasized in this chapter, beginning to hope — that is, moving into connection — can be terrifying. All one's old fears are reawakened. It means defying the past.

To summarize, the key component in the process of moving from disconnection to new connection in therapy is the therapist's empathic resonance with both sides of the paradox in the patient and in herself. This resonance moves the patient to begin gradually to bring more and more of herself into the therapy relationship. In particular, it is essential that the therapist stay in touch with the patient's terror of giving up old strategies.

10

JOAN'S STORY

━━

We have been describing the central themes in our relational model of therapy — moving from disconnection to new connection, empathically resonating with a range of strategies of disconnection, and examining the development of relational images and their meanings.

We would like now to illustrate this model more fully by addressing all of these issues in the work with a woman one of us has seen over several years. Through following the process over the long term we can better convey the layers and complexities of this kind of therapeutic work. The progress is not linear, but rather flows back and forth between moving toward connection and turning to disconnection and then moving again toward more connection.[1]

━━

Joan, a forty-three-year-old woman, entered therapy because of depression. She was troubled and worried about ending up in an empty house in the near future because she anticipated that her youngest daughter would be leaving home for college the following year.

Joan had grown up in a family of modest means. There were frequent moves and money was always an issue. She married young and had been divorced for many years, supporting herself and her four children with very little help from her ex-husband. Although Joan had many acquaintances, neighbors, and colleagues, she had no good friends. Despite a pleasant social manner, she distanced herself from people and told me that she preferred to be by herself and with her children.

I soon learned that although she was respectful of her father, Joan felt contempt for her mother, whom she saw as completely incompetent and unresponsive, without any personality. She found it almost impossible to discuss anything with her mother because her mother was so silent. In all the years of raising her children, Joan had never thought of calling her mother for advice since she seemed to her so inadequate, so anxious and "pathetic." In contrast to what she described as her mother's incompetence, Joan had developed a strategy of self-sufficiency and independence.

I often felt moved by how hard the early years of the marriage had been for Joan. Her husband had been very withdrawn and rarely at home, and she felt she had raised her children alone. She was ashamed of not always knowing how to manage them and was fearful of revealing any sign of her self-doubt, lest people be contemptuous of her.

Joan expressed surprise that I somehow knew how hard it had been for her all those years and that I truly appreciated why it was so awful to be so isolated and alone. Slowly, she began to express much more sadness about these years, but this made her feel very uncomfortable. While I was very encouraged by her feeling and showing her sadness, she hated this self-image. It meant to her that she was weak, and that no one would want to be with her. I told her that I thought that her ability to know her feelings more fully and to risk bringing them into therapy marked an important shift, namely, that she was beginning to express more aspects of herself. My reframing the meaning and value of this expression of her sadness was perplexing to her, but it clearly also captured her interest.

I wondered why Joan hadn't made friendships with her neighbors or with the women with whom she worked. I did notice, however, that she was consistently contemptuous of them and dissociated herself from them. She was startled and even shocked when I asked her why she was so demeaning of other women when she was a woman herself. She said she had truly not realized that she carried the unspoken assumption "I'm not one of them!" when she was with other women. This realization turned out to be a big moment for her, and she returned to it periodically.

RELATIONAL IMAGES

Only after talking about how hard it was to feel so isolated and alone for so long could Joan begin to articulate some of her relational images. I noted that she seemed to feel that if she ever needed someone, no one would be there. I wondered with her, too, if that expectation didn't feel so awful that she did not even want to try to reach out to someone for help. This led to a series of memories and associations which she said were about her mother, but were in fact about both parents. In one memory she saw herself at age seven, sitting in the back seat of her parent's car en route to the hospital where she was to have surgery. She recalled saying, "I'm not afraid to die." And no one said a word. She had no memory of being frightened, just the awfulness of the silence that followed. I was very moved by this image of Joan as a little girl and felt her terror. I shared this with her and I believe I conveyed my own sad feelings about her experience. Although this story about the hospital was an old memory, it was the first time Joan had been able to articulate how scared she "must have been," yet when she first told me about it she could not *feel* the terror. Nor could she experience any compassion for what it really had been like for her.

Joan brought many such poignant images into therapy, but usually without the powerful feelings that probably had originally accompanied them. I told her that perhaps it had been too dangerous at the time to feel her longings and terror or to speak about them. Only later could she return to some of these early scenes and finally experience the deep pain that they had originally caused her.

THE CENTRAL RELATIONAL PARADOX

Other, similar memories emerged, all illustrating the central relational paradox. These memories showed how profoundly disconnected Joan felt from both parents and how she had tried to protect herself from these painful disconnections through her strategies of keeping distant and "not needing anyone." These memories led us to talk about how whenever she tried to make a connection, her attempts would "fall on the floor." This "falling on the floor" image became an ongoing metaphor, and we used it to identify the many moments in Joan's past and current life when she expected that no one would "pick up" on her feelings, that her feelings would be ignored or dismissed. As we saw together how frequently this negative expectation emerged, we could name this pervasive relational image and begin to learn where it came from and what impact it had on her life.

In her work with me, for example, Joan found herself unable to acknowledge my responsiveness to her experience. She could note it and at the same time want to insist that my facial expression was blank, even though she also "knew" it wasn't. This was very perplexing to her since she prided herself on being rational and fair, and could not understand her apparent resistance to taking in how different I was from her expectations. I saw this as an example of her transference to me, and it helped me appreciate how awful it felt when she could not believe that I could be responsive to her.

This discrepancy between what she "knew" about me and how she experienced me in our sessions ultimately led us both to a new level of appreciation and respect for the power of her early relational images, and how strongly she held on to them even if they no longer fit her current situation. However, even as we were working on this issue Joan also began to notice other features of her relational interactions and gradually began to shift her behavior. For example, as she became more attentive to interactions with women, she began to see that underlying her contempt for them was her fear that they would not like her, would exclude her. She saw that she was always on the verge of panic if she accepted an invitation to be with other women socially, for fear that she would not look just right, not "be perfect." It was easier to make an excuse and not go at all. But now she saw that it was her terror of not being accepted rather than her contempt for these women that kept her at a distance.

EMPATHIC RESONANCE WITH STRATEGIES

I think Joan was able to move toward this new understanding because I had been able to feel empathic with her need to be contemptuous of other women — knowing at the same time that this attitude kept her isolated. But I did try to honor her strategies of disconnection. I saw this dynamic as another example of the central relational paradox. She had to negate her yearnings for connection with other women, so she developed strategies of disconnection, that is, contempt for other women, in order to ward off her expectation that no one would like her or accept her. Here, as always, the important question was not what was "wrong" with Joan because she couldn't seem to get along with other women; rather the question was, How did Joan's difficulties with women cover up her deeper yearnings for, and fears of, connection — yearnings which had been so threatening in the past?

A great deal of the work in therapy is this kind of attention to the different relational images a person carries with her. But what really moves the therapy is the therapist's energetic participation with her patient in trying to articulate these images and how they feel, particularly as these images are played out through the transference in the therapy relationship. For example, as Joan and I were moving toward greater connection, she would express her anger toward me from time to time as a way of distancing from me, but her anger confused her because it didn't seem reasonable. In time, she was able to gain more clarity. It became more apparent to both of us that her anger was aroused whenever she became more aware of the importance of a particular relationship; her anger then would serve as a strategy of disconnection, distancing her from me and other relationships.

At one point Joan developed some medical problems that were alarming. Unfortunately, I was going on vacation during the time that she would be learning more about how serious these symptoms were. Before I went away I told her how bad I felt that I could not be with her during this time, and that I was concerned that she might move back into her more distancing strategies as a consequence. She was very open to discussing this issue and seemed very mindful of this pattern. Yet when I saw her for the first time after my vacation, I felt I was seeing her through a telescope — she seemed to be literally miles away. She announced at the outset of this session that she had not thought about therapy at all while I was gone, that she had managed to cope with her health difficulties very well and really did not have much more to report. When I told her how it felt to be with her, and reminded her of what we had discussed before I left, she was truly startled. Because this theme of distance was so central to the work we had been doing for some time, Joan and I were able to move back into connection again in a very short time. In fact, we both felt we had learned more powerfully than before how terrifying it had always been for her to allow herself to be vulnerable in the face of her expectation that no one would respond to her.

UNDERLYING CONSTRUCTS

Just as the therapist tries to identify patterns of relational images that keep a person out of connection, she also attends to the accompanying meanings, the constructions the person develops about these images. Joan expressed confusion as well as anger toward her mother for not being responsive to her. When I first asked her why she thought her mother was so unresponsive, she expressed bewilderment and frustration. As an adolescent, she had tried to ask her father why her mother wasn't responsive, but he had said that it would be disloyal to talk about her mother, and besides, "she was a saint." These kinds of statements by Joan's father powerfully reinforced her construction that something must really be wrong with *her.*

This construction was supported by a family story. When Joan was an infant, she suddenly stopped eating and had to be hospitalized for a week. In growing up, she periodically had "difficulty eating," had upset stomachs and other kinds of intestinal distress that were very upsetting to her mother. This story led Joan to the firm belief that she was a bad child, a person who was unlovable because she could not accept love, could not show her mother that she loved her through expressing a desire and pleasure in being fed. She held on to this belief with great tenacity and was sure it was true. Yet at the same time, she was also amazed to see how powerful this belief was and how she resisted changing it, despite her growing awareness in our work together that there were other ways to understand what had happened. One of the most poignant images she brought to therapy was of herself sitting in the front seat of a car, her father driving, her mother next to him, and she wedged between her mother and the window. She recalls imagining that there was a faucet over her heart that would carry love to her mother. She simply reported this, but had no memory of how she had felt or what it conveyed. I asked her if the faucet also went the other way, her mother sending her love to her. She looked completely startled, became upset, and stated unequivocally that she never would have wanted that, not at all, and couldn't talk about this image further at that time.

What we learned over time together was that as a young child, Joan had been unable to make sense out of her mother's lack of responsiveness to her; it had been terribly hard for her to find out anything about how her mother felt about anything. I felt in touch with how awful it is not to understand the important people in our lives, how painful it was for Joan to feel her mother was inaccessible to her, and how alone she was in trying to make sense out of her relationships. I could readily resonate with her anguish when she was able to express how painfully perplexed she felt. She would say, with intense expressions of her frustration and exasperation, "I want to *know* what happened. *Why* was my mother so unable to say anything? Did something *happen* to her? Why couldn't she *respond* to me? What was the *matter* with her?" It was almost easier to have a concrete explanation of why things "fell on the floor" as a result of any expression of her feelings — that is, it was easier for her to feel that she was bad and unlovable than to stay with the confusion and anxiety associated with not understanding.

We think Joan was expressing the terrible confusion all children must feel when they cannot understand why their parents and other adults are behaving in ways that feel so hurtful. This confusion is exquisitely painful for the child as she searches for some understanding to allay her terrors. As a child Joan could reach only very simple explanations, namely that she must have made her mother angry because she could not eat, and thus was an unlovable child.

SALIENT FEATURES IN THE FAMILY

Some of the salient features leading to disconnections in families that we discussed in Chapter 5 were apparent in Joan's family. Her mother was certainly inaccessible emotionally and Joan had a sense that there were secrets that she could never be privy to. She always believed that her parents were not telling her some important fact about her mother. Joan's view of her mother as incompetent led her to try to make some connection with her through taking charge of many household tasks. Particularly in adolescence, Joan also tried to teach her mother how to do certain things, like shaving her legs or putting on makeup, but she would "make a mess of it" and couldn't accept Joan's help. Joan then felt even more contemptuous of her mother, on the one hand, and rejected and pushed away, on the other. As an adult, Joan's major way of "connecting" with her mother was to do chores for her, shopping for food or driving her places, but her mother never thanked her or acknowledged what she had done.

The awfulness of Joan's early years of feeling so alone and unworthy began to break through her guarded and nonemotional veneer. At such times during a therapy session, she would begin to feel panicky and terrified that she was no longer in control of her feelings. I told her that I thought she was making some important steps forward in her recognition of how awful it had been for her, feeling it probably more directly and intensely than she ever had before. I shared my notion that when she was a child she must have felt too vulnerable to let this pain into awareness, since she had not had the capabilities yet to tolerate these feelings and she was so alone with them. I said that now that she was an adult, she was, in fact, more capable of bearing her pain, and — most important — she did not have to do so alone.

SHIFTS IN PERCEPTION OF MOTHER

The next phase of our work was to address Joan's constructions more directly. As an adult, she could begin to see the other people in her life in a broader context, to gain a new perspective on her mother's behavior. In the process, Joan began, almost inadvertently it seemed, to bring in stories about her mother, which allowed me to see her mother in a more complicated way. Instead of descriptions of her as a passive, silent, pathetic, empty person, I began to hear remarks about her humor and about how others saw her as a "sweet" person.

When I pointed these remarks out, Joan felt uncomfortable, told me she didn't like me to notice them. While she knew she had a strong resistance to my raising questions about her one-dimensional negative view of her mother, she was not sure why. As we puzzled about this together, she said she wanted to hold on to her anger toward her mother because without that anger she was left with a horrible feeling of anguish. Anguish was the feeling she could most readily identify when she began to feel the pain of her deep sense of disconnection from her mother. The reasons for this anguish became more clear as she moved first into a recognition of this disconnection and then into the belief that she could never have an impact on her mother, that she probably would never find out what happened between her and her mother. I was very moved by how awful it felt to come to this realization. In this context, she began to talk about her mother as old and frail, and about how she could not bear the thought that her mother might die before she could ever find out how her mother felt about her or why her mother could not love her.

It was her ability to identify this anguish, and to see how painful and powerful it was, that led Joan to relate another image. This was the first time she directly revealed her longing for her mother. Her mother had told her about this event; Joan herself had only a dim memory of it. When her mother came home after giving birth to her younger brother, Joan began to run excitedly around the bed, each time touching her mother's hand and running around again. She remembered she had been looking out of the window waiting for the car that was bringing her mother home. When I said, "I never heard that story before," she said, "I didn't want to tell you." When I wondered why, she said, "It would show a chink in my armor. It's too humiliating. I cannot bear to be vulnerable — I cannot bear that you will see me that way and lose respect for me." Joan had reached the point where she could actually articulate her construction that for her to reveal any yearning for her mother or anyone else meant she was utterly worthless, not warranting respect.

MOVEMENT IN THERAPY

This was a time of enormous movement in our work, which ultimately led to Joan's recognition that to see her mother as a more complicated person might open up her own yearnings for closeness with her mother, which were still terrifying. It was the beginning of her facing her vulnerability — and more fully representing herself. During this period, Joan's mother became ill and had to be hospitalized. At first Joan moved into the caretaking role, as a way to have some connection with her mother, but without feeling anything for her. She used her strategy of emotional disengagement to distance herself from her mother but at the same time became obsessed with doing everything perfectly for her. She had to buy the perfect bed jacket, and send the nicest plant, and the like. But again, her mother never acknowledged these efforts.

Joan became increasingly aware of how hurt she felt when her mother did not seem to acknowledge her. She would tell me how anxious she became when she had to visit her at the hospital, fearful that no one else would be there and she wouldn't know what to say to her mother; but if her father and brother or other family members were there, she could not bear to see her mother talking to them and never addressing Joan directly. When I asked her what her mother talked about with other visitors, she was surprised to find that she had no idea. She realized that she couldn't listen because she was so sure her mother was being much more responsive to other people than she could be to Joan.

Joan then began to examine the ways she might have pushed her mother away through the years; she wondered if her mother might have been intimidated by her "forcefulness" and her critical view of her mother — whether she might have "come on too strong."

Joan was surprised to see how the nursing staff at the hospital treated her mother. They thought she was very courageous and responded to her with affection and respect. Gradually, Joan began to feel more empathic with her mother's life. In this setting, her father's domination and control over what her mother did or said became more apparent. As she tried harder to engage with her mother, she saw her mother trying to respond more directly to her but then being repeatedly cut off by her father. When Joan's mother returned home from the hospital, Joan and her children began to visit more often. She noticed how much her father needed to be the center of attention. On one occasion when there was animated conversation she saw her father looking annoyed, sulking in a corner of the room, not talking to anyone.

Her mother continued to be difficult to engage at times, was often silent, and consistently deferred to Joan's father, but there were clear qualitative changes in her relationship with Joan. Once her mother amazed her by noting what a beautiful sunset she had seen the previous evening and then said, "I could leave this world more easily in such a wonderful setting." Joan was very moved and could begin to feel her sadness about seeing her mother's fragility and realizing that she was "getting ready to die."

In our sessions, Joan began to talk with much more feeling about how much she wanted from her mother and how little her mother was able to give to her. One day she told me that she saw "the look of love for me in my mother's eyes." I was surprised to hear her say this and asked her when she had noted that. She said, "I always knew it; but I couldn't bear to say it, because then it would really have been all my fault." But another reason she could not admit seeing that look in her mother's eyes was that it pained her so that her mother could not show her love more fully and more concretely, that she could never show any physical affection to her children or grandchildren. Joan could then begin to talk about her longings to be hugged, held by her mother.

Joan had moved an enormous distance in shifting from the compelling belief or construction that she was the bad child who could not love, to feeling like a very sad child who was not given the kind of love that could have helped her feel worthwhile and able to develop good feelings about sincerely caring for her mother. For the first time she could feel some self-empathy.[2] Joan's constructions of the meanings of her relational images had shifted to become more multifaceted assessments of herself and other people; these assessments were much less harsh than before, but they also confronted her with people's limitations.

A SHIFT IN PERSPECTIVE

The next part of our work was to deal with the grief Joan began to experience in the face of her inability to gain access to her mother while growing up. Seeing her mother in context certainly helped her to let go of her contemptuous attitudes and other strategies of disconnection that pushed her mother away, but she needed to come to terms with the limits of her relationship with her mother.

I will not describe this work except to say that Joan could move into it because she was now much more in touch with her own feelings — and with me. Her new perspective, however, was very freeing for Joan, and this was especially evident in her interactions with her children. She had always tried to be responsive to her children, to be different from her mother, but she now realized that often what she was doing was attempting to please them, to avoid conflict, to make sure they would not want to distance themselves from her. She was gradually more able to address the difficulties that arose in her relationships with her children, to acknowledge differences between them, and to move into more authentic connection with them.

This account reflects some important aspects of our work together, but certainly not all of them. Many other themes were explored, and we did a lot of significant work on Joan's problematic relationships with the men in her family, her ex-husband and her father, and on other areas of her life.

We have focused on Joan's struggles with her mother because they illustrate many of the points we wanted to make. But her mother's relationship with her father clearly had a major impact on Joan; despite Joan's criticism of her mother's passivity and apparent incompetence, she also became painfully aware of how demeaning her father was toward her mother. So we do not see Joan's mother as the "core" or basis of Joan's difficulties. Rather, the relationship between Joan and her mother needs to be seen in the context of her family and of the larger culture.

Joan's response to reading this presentation of her story helped further enlarge our understanding of our work. She was very moved by our interest in the whole process of her growth and change, and she felt that she had been able to give something back in this way. She hoped it would help other women as well. She then added that for her one of the major consequences of this work was her growing capacity to be empathic, that the positive changes in her relationships with her mother, even with all its limitations, and with her children, friends, and others were largely due to her ability to understand them better in a deep, emotional way.

We have described the work with Joan in such detail in order to convey a more concrete sense of what we actually do in trying to work in a relational way, and specifically how our notions about the central relational paradox, the strategies of disconnection, and relational images and their meanings inform our work.

Many of the things I said in this example might be called interpretations in traditional therapy, but we do not think of them in this sense. We see our communications as therapists as part of the ongoing dialogue or *relational movement*. They are the therapist's questions, hunches, feelings — responses. They are important if they help to create the flow, the ongoing interaction that leads to the kind of connection in which therapist and patient together come to the deeper understanding that allows change. The therapist does not lend the patient understanding; she offers the responsiveness of her thoughts and feelings. This responsiveness leads to the movement toward greater connection. It is this increased connection that makes it possible for patients to experience more fully and deeply the profoundly important aspects of their experience that they have had to keep out of connection.

SUMMING UP

We believe that the centerpiece of psychotherapy is the creation of a new relationship — a relationship in which the patient can include more of herself, that is, more of her experience and of her feelings about that experience, the parts she has had to keep out of relationships in the past.

As we have suggested, throughout the course of therapy the therapist must continually focus on how connected or disconnected she feels with each person and must also remain empathic with both sides of the central relational paradox, that is, both the desire for connection and the strategies for disconnection.

Only as the therapist does this can therapist and patient together begin to perceive the relational images and meanings that have guided the patient's life. Many of the feelings these contain are extremely painful, too painful to explore without another person who can resonate with them and respond to them.

As patient and therapist unpeel the layers of relational images and their meanings, the patient can begin to glimpse the possibility of different meanings. These possibilities open up the path to the creation of different relationships and to a different image of herself. She can move out of repetitive, constricting strategies of disconnection and into new connections that are mutually empathic and mutually empowering.

Thus we have seen both patients and therapists bring their growth in connection to other relationships in the world. They can begin to engage with others with deeper empathy, and this helps create a greater sense of community in small and large ways. We will be illustrating this movement in the last chapter.

PART FOUR

COMMUNITY

11

FROM SELF TO COMMUNITY
IN THERAPY, IN LIFE

THERAPY IN CONNECTION

While we believe deeply in trying to demystify ideas about psychological development and the process of therapy, we do not mean to suggest that therapy is simple or easy. When people need therapy, they need a therapist who has learned a great deal about participating in its complexities. Therapists need to acquire a critical knowledge of an extensive body of literature on psychological development and psychological problems. They also need intensive clinical training and work with supervisors and peers. Learning to *move in relationship* — to facilitate the patient's difficult movement away from the strategies of disconnection through the uncertainties of vulnerability and on to new connections — is demanding and difficult.

It is therefore troubling when we hear of the ways in which our perspective has been misunderstood. For example, several more traditional therapists have said that what we propose is that a person need simply be "kind" or "nice" in order to do therapy. And unfortunately there are some therapists who believe that our emphasis on empathy and relationships means that being "nice" and "caring" is the same thing as conducting effective psychotherapy. Empathy does not mean "being nice." It means trying to be with the truth of another person's experience in all its many facets.

Equal in importance to clinical training and academic preparation for therapy is an understanding of the larger relational context in which therapy occurs. Our relational view leads us to a new perspective, a different concept about therapy's connection to the larger world. In our view, both patient and therapist have developed within a culture that has deprived all of us of fully growth-fostering relationships, but they are coming together to try to create something different, something that runs counter to the damaging effects of the larger society. Both patient and therapist are engaged in a creative act of healing and empowerment. It is a part of a larger effort of trying to understand deeply how our surrounding conditions affect us all.

As we said in Chapter 7, in order to be able to work in this way — to try to be present and truly resonant and responsive to another person — the therapist cannot be a removed, omniscient person. It has become clear to us that therapists need a larger relational network that helps them stay in connection through many of the profoundly moving experiences they have in therapy. We think all therapists need to participate in ongoing groups of colleagues with whom they can share their experiences, especially those that are problematic and painful.

Patients, too, need a surrounding context of relationships in addition to therapy. If they have family and friends who can engage in mutual ways, they are fortunate. Many people don't have enough of these opportunities, but other kinds of relationships are now available in many locations, in the mutual help groups modeled after Alcoholics Anonymous, for instance. These groups can often provide powerful connections and validation that are different from anything therapy can offer. We believe that it is the mutual empathy and mutual empowerment that these groups foster that make them effective. Women often find the groups that have learned from feminist criticism and have changed their language and procedures to reflect the truth of women's experience to be the most helpful of these.[1]

Recent articles criticizing many kinds of mutual help groups fail to distinguish the valuable from the distorted; they reveal a lack of contact with the many people who have experienced the powerful beneficial effects of some of these groups. While it is true that anything can be commercialized, trivialized, or coopted away from its original intent, we believe that some recent writers have underestimated the profound help that can be provided by a good mutual help group.

In addition to twelve-step and related programs, there are many other kinds of groups and workshops that can benefit women in particular. Some concentrate on specific issues or problems, some on specific life events, such as widowhood or aging. Women have also joined together to help each other in groups for mothers of young children or for women dealing with divorce or other issues. Some offer a direct link to action that has an impact on larger public policy issues and societal conditions. For example, some battered women's programs help women directly and also work on the larger scene and have stimulated many (but not yet all) necessary changes in legislation, the courts, the police, and hospitals. (Because of this climate, national and state medical societies have at long last launched campaigns to educate doctors in recognizing and treating battered women.)

There are many forms of therapy that can be very helpful — such as group therapy, couples therapy, or family therapy. It's a question of what's right for each person and what may be right at different points in that person's journey. One person found profound change in a mothers and daughters group, another in a group for mothers of children whose fathers had sexually abused the children. There are many other examples. We believe that it is part of our responsibility as therapists to tell people about other resources. (Many times patients have found out about them and informed us.)

In saying that relational therapy on a one-to-one basis leads patient and therapist to become more connected and to create together an empowering relationship, we do not suggest that this turns therapy into another kind of relationship, such as friendship or a family relationship; rather, it turns therapy into better therapy.

Therapy is a relationship in its own right, a specially designed relationship intended to help the patient work on finding a way through disconnections to new connections, first with the therapist and then with other people. As we've said, if we appreciate the power of the forces that lead to disconnections, we can understand that therapy can be intense and difficult; if we understand the empowerment of connections, we know how it can be extraordinarily fulfilling. Therapists must try to make therapy strengthening and empowering through the difficult times. This requires special "working conditions."

Therapy takes place when a person is going through a difficult time. Friends and family, if available, have not been able to help enough; something different is needed. A more specific kind of movement in relationship has to be provided, something that is not the same as what occurs with friends or family members.

A special framework for this relationship has to be constructed and protected. So far as we have been able to figure it out, therapy cannot usually include the kind of activities that people expect from family, friends, or coworkers. For example, people often have a right to expect friends or family to pitch in and help with practical matters in dealing with many life issues, such as an illness in the family or finding a job. In the usual course of things, however, this is not something a therapist would do. Indeed, if the therapist did, it might shift the focus from the ongoing psychological work. The therapist's task is to maintain a psychological perspective at these times. For example, in looking for a job, a patient may need to work with the therapist to sort out and clarify choices and their psychological meanings or to deal with anxieties, inhibitions, and the like. However, if the therapist steps in and takes action, she or he risks influencing the patient's choice too much. At other times, patients will not yet be able to tell the therapist that they dislike or disagree with the therapist's actions or advice. The latter situation sets up a hidden source of conflict and disconnection that interferes with the optimal progression of therapy. In some particular instances outside events may intrude on the therapy relationship and become unavoidable. Most important in these instances, as in everything, is that therapist and patient try to discuss these issues together.

Patients are often curious about their therapists and may also wish to be with them in different ways outside of therapy. We believe the patient has a right to know about the therapist's approach and values as well as his or her background and training. Further, the desire to know even more about the therapist makes sense and can be discussed. While we believe that therapists should have *only* the therapy relationship and no other with their patients, patient and therapist should examine together all of these other desires. (In the past, and often still, some therapists have made patients feel deeply embarrassed and ashamed about their need for information or about their curiosity or wishes; they often "interpreted" them in ways that made people feel they were not legitimate: "I wonder why you're asking these questions. They seem to be a way of avoiding your own problems," or, even worse, "It seems you have very prominent voyeuristic impulses.")

We see questions about the therapist as part of everyone's struggle to find connection intertwined with legitimate fears of that connection. In the face of these fears, the patient needs to know who the therapist truly is as a person. We have not found that discussing these wishes interferes with exploring the transference, as discussed in Chapter 7.

We do not believe, however, that the therapist should bring his or her life issues into the therapy, nor that the patient should take care of the therapist or be responsible for the therapist's needs. We do know that patients may want to do some or all of these things for their therapists. There are important reasons to honor this desire, only one of which is that it may reflect a patient's feelings of inequality at not being able to help the therapist and always being in the "helpee" position. (This issue is often particularly significant for people who were very parentified as children.) All of these issues are important to understand; all should be acknowledged and discussed within the context of the ongoing therapy.

In fact, however, therapy is the one relationship in which the patient should not have to worry about, or be burdened by, another person's issues. Also, after therapy ends the therapist can still be available, to be contacted if problems emerge in the future, but the relationship continues to be defined by the structure of therapy, not by the kinds of personal considerations that characterize friendships or family relationships.

Similarly, when we talk about the therapist stretching and enlarging, we mean that all mutually empathic and mutually empowering relationships are going to enlarge any of us by virtue of our participation in them. However, the purpose of the therapeutic relationship is *not* the therapist's growth. The purpose is the patient's movement toward less suffering and a more fulfilling life. The therapist's responsibility is always to work toward making it possible for the patient to bring more of her or his experience into the relationship and to engage with the patient about that experience.

We believe that the most important point is that the therapist *be there psychologically* with the patient in a *real* way. This is essential for therapy; otherwise a person cannot focus on deeply painful experience and cannot put herself in such a place of exposure and risk. As we discussed in Chapter 7, "being there psychologically" means trying to engage in the process of mutual empathy. This engagement includes trying to understand what the patient is experiencing and going *with* the patient through the range of painful and difficult thoughts and feelings that arise. As we've tried to convey, this is not a one-time occurrence, but happens often as patient and therapist move through periods of disconnection to new connection, and empathy is especially crucial since the initial harm was in the very fact of being alone and powerless in past disconnecting or violating experiences.[2]

Because our hope here is to sketch the guiding framework of the approach we have been evolving for therapy, we are not attempting to cover all of its parameters. There are many other features of therapy that we consider genuine dilemmas, not the least of which are time (scheduling), money, and other power differentials in the therapy relationship. All of these and more require extensive consideration. The larger culture affects all of these factors and has influenced the prevalent ways of thinking about them, as have the more immediate impinging factors such as the state of health and mental health care systems in this country. For example, in public and private practice situations we ask patients to pay for therapy. There ought to be provision for everyone to get the help they need regardless of their economic circumstances. The present arrangement clearly reflects our economic system and is not an optimal situation. In recent years, profit-making insurance plans have limited therapy drastically. This trend represents a major problem.

Further, we believe that there are enormous differences in power within the therapy relationship. This power differential sets up similar dynamics as those found in other "helper-helpee" relationships, such as teacher-student, doctor-patient, parent-child. Beyond these lie others that are even more augmented in therapy. For example, patients are asked to reveal their deepest and most painful thoughts and feelings; the therapist is not. The fact that the patient is exposed and vulnerable in a way the therapist is not creates a serious difference in power. As we've discussed, we do believe that bringing these painful parts of experience into relationship and finding that they lead to more connection is the essence of the therapeutic process, but we would like to find ways that patients — and in turn, the patient-therapist relationship — did not have to suffer from the power differential while we are working toward this goal.

While we have not found ways to change this situation that fully satisfy us, we do think certain steps can be useful. The first is that the therapist be aware of this power differential and its impact on the patient and on the therapeutic process. Therapists' awareness can lead to the fullest possible discussion of the issue; again, this discussion should occur not once, but repeatedly when the issue arises in various forms throughout therapy.

Our second general notion is that therapists must guide all of their actions toward moving toward mutual empowerment. In other words, the goal is full mutuality and equality of power and the therapist's task is to work toward that goal. Saying this does not take care of the problem, because the therapist still has more power along the way and to that extent the patient is still at the mercy of the therapist. The movement from inequality of power to equality is not a form of activity that our culture has developed or described optimally. We've begun a description of how we're trying to find the path in therapy but it is not totally satisfactory.

Certainly, our views have evolved over time and will change further as we work to make therapy even more relational.

FROM SELF TO COMMUNITY

As we have suggested earlier, when a person moves into more authentic connection with the therapist and also with other people in her life, she finds more connection with her own experience. Feeling that another person can be with her, she can bear to see the truth of what happened to her in the past and can become much more empathic and understanding of herself.

When we do not have to be occupied with being vigilant, protecting our strategies for disconnection, we can truly feel more deeply joined with others in their experiences, both distressing and joyful. We can allow our desire for connection to flow more freely and find others who meet us in this desire.

In the end, finding one's own path to connection leads to finding a sense of larger community. As we come to know the truth of our own very particular experiences of disconnection, we can come to know how we all suffer from the forces of disconnection. This sense of a shared experience leads many people to want to work to change the conditions that create damaging disconnections in the world. And, in doing so, people can have the pleasure of seeing their impact on others and on the larger social or political scene — no longer powerless or victims, but participants in the world.

It is not that we as therapists ever use therapy to tell people what to do, politically or otherwise. Rather, we see that people often find the kind of action that is most meaningful to them, the kind for which they are most motivated and effective. It is a wonderful step to be able to move on from a restricted world, with its unchanging limits and replications of old ways of being, to a world of connections with others that open out to new possibilities.

This moving into fuller connection can happen at different levels, from the most immediate and personal to larger institutional settings and broader political and social contexts. Many of our patients have demonstrated a great generosity of spirit, and more faith in themselves and other people, as they have gradually given up their strategies of disconnection and risked fuller participation in the world. We'll offer some examples.

In the early stages of therapy with Joan, the woman described in Chapter 10, she demonstrated an obsessive preoccupation with herself. She described her constant vigilance about how others were treating her and desperately held on to her strategies for survival, which kept her isolated and feeling alone in the world. Paradoxically, as she could begin to name the things that really mattered to her and to feel that they were important and legitimate, she became more aware of other people in a different way. For example, previously she would spend a lot of time on her appearance, feeling that she needed always to be perfectly "turned out" to be acceptable. She was, however, also self-critical about her intense concern with appearance; she thought it meant that she must be a shallow person. She began to see how much this concern depleted her energy, leaving her little room to be attentive to others or to "be herself." Joan's shift from self-absorption due to painful relational images and constructions of self-blame, to increased empathic awareness of self and others, allowed her to move more fully into the world.[3] During this process, she began to take the risk of building a more intimate relationship with a man. She would find herself moving toward him and then mobilizing some of her old strategies of disconnection. One day she came to therapy quite exhilarated, and said that the day before, "a light bulb went on inside of me as I realized that being in a relationship was really better than being alone." And she added, "I never thought I would be able to admit that."

Another woman, Diane, described a very grim childhood. Her mother was depressed and very critical; her father abandoned the family when Diane was six years old, and she believed that one of her mother's boyfriends probably molested her shortly after her father left. In our work together, Diane could not experience any empathy for herself as a child. Once she brought in some pictures of herself in which she looked very sad. When I remarked about that and tried to resonate with how painful her childhood had been, she became irritated with me. She could only be critical of this little girl; she hated those sad pictures because she felt she looked like such a "wimp" as a child. She believed it was impossible to love someone who looked so unhappy and unresponsive. Although over time she softened some in response to her experience of herself as a child, she continued to hold on to the belief that she was to blame for the bad things that happened to her.

During the course of therapy, Diane retired from her job as a lab technician and decided to do some volunteer work with very young children. It was this experience that made the difference in Diane's ability to be more empathic with her own history and experience. She was surprised, herself, that she was drawn to volunteering in a group home for children who had terrible histories of violence, sexual abuse, and abandonment. She found herself very much drawn to these children and for the first time could empathize with her own experiences as a very unhappy little girl. She began to talk about how innocent these children seemed, and how tragic that they were so alone in the world. Diane began to wonder how she could make a difference in these children's lives, even if she was at the group home just a few days each week. Her work with these children and the joy she experienced when some of them greeted her with excitement and affection was extremely empowering for her, not only in that setting but in all her relationships.

Our colleague Janet Surrey has told of Cora, who was raped by a patient while working as a psychiatric nurse. She moved through a long period of terror, shame, and isolation. Through her work in psychotherapy and in a group with other rape victims, Cora began to acknowledge her fear, vulnerability, and anger. She joined with other women to speak out publicly about her experience in lectures and in testimony before legislative committees. She was also able to include a discussion of this subject in the nursing education curriculum. Her experience became a resource for empowering herself and others. She came to appreciate that her experience was not an isolated event, but rather one shared, directly and indirectly, with other women.[4]

In another example, Vicky, who had spent much of her life in isolation, insisting for a long time that she preferred solitude to being with people, began to notice some dramatic differences in her day-to-day experience. On just one day she noted three remarkable events. She had learned that morning that her group therapist had just had a baby; she was pleased that all was well and found herself experiencing warm and caring feelings for this woman. She had the thought that she would like to send flowers but began to worry whether that was "appropriate"; instead of obsessing about it as she would have done in the past, she decided that she would just do it. And it gave her great pleasure.

Later that day at work, Vicky heard someone playing beautiful music on the violin. It occurred to her that the person playing might be a certain student she knew only slightly. This student had once told her about her own struggle to overcome major obstacles that had interfered with her ability to play for some time. Vicky followed the sound of the violin until she reached a large room, and there she saw the student, deeply engrossed in playing. She had the urge to go up to her and tell her what pleasure she felt in hearing her play again and so beautifully. For a brief moment she held back, fearful, as always, that she would make an unwanted intrusion. Again she resisted those thoughts and went forward to express her pleasure. The student's big smile and appreciation were very moving and empowering for her.

Finally, she passed someone in the corridor whom she knew but saw as a very powerful figure, someone she would not ordinarily approach. Yet she had heard him being interviewed on the radio the previous day and very much appreciated what he had said. She decided to stop him and tell him how much she enjoyed the interview. He was, of course, delighted, and he engaged her in an energetic conversation. These three events, although seemingly small, were amazing accomplishments for this woman, who had risked a great deal to follow through on her sincere wishes to join with these three people in an important way; and she had clearly had a positive impact on each of them. Vicky's earlier relational images would have informed her that her feelings and thoughts would not matter to anyone and that if she tried to express them, she would be humiliated and dismissed.

Several years after she ended therapy, Clara, the woman described in Chapter 7, became interested in understanding more about women's experience in general. In the context of her work situation, she began to interview women from a range of social, educational, and economic backgrounds, taping these interviews and hoping to derive from them a landscape of perspectives to help all women validate their own experiences.

Through the course of therapy, another woman, Phyllis, began to gain increasing recognition at work as she moved from a more retiring and accommodating stance to one in which she became more able to express her ideas and to risk representing herself and her talents more fully. This was very different from her story when she began therapy; then, she'd had little self-confidence, and if she thought anyone was being critical of her she would quickly retreat into despair and resentment. Now, she was engaged in trying to create a mutually empathic and empowering atmosphere with her bosses, her peers, and those she was supervising. At a stressful time within the institution in which she worked (morale was very low due to lay-offs) there was considerable tension between people at different levels of power. She was able to let her boss know how hard it must be for him to have everyone angry at him but she told him that she thought he could make a difference if he more actively engaged with his employees and listened to their concerns.

Phyllis created a forum for meeting with all the people involved and facilitated an energetic exchange among them. In the process, she encouraged her boss to be responsive to his staff through "not being defensive" and letting them know he did not have all the answers but truly wanted them to participate in the company's problem-solving endeavors. As a result, he created a task force that consisted of employees at different levels who could bring their voices into this work setting and could feel they were having an impact on the way decisions were made. People responded with energy and high motivation, and morale was greatly improved. We know that even this much opportunity is not available in most work settings, but the point is that this woman was able to find a way to make a significant difference in her whole work climate.

Phyllis was not aware that she was bringing what she had learned in her own therapy into the work situation. But as we discussed it, she was gratified to see how much she had created a kind of "family setting" at work that was strikingly different from her own family background. Phyllis had grown up in a large family. Her father labored very hard as a farmer while her mother worked the late shift at a factory, to help make ends meet. Both parents were quite authoritarian, and rules were very strict and inflexible. Phyllis's relational images that she could never be heard, that her point of view would always be dismissed, and that conflict had to be avoided at all costs kept her relatively immobilized for a long time. In the course of therapy, Phyllis was often very moved by feeling heard and recognized for the first time, and she learned the enormous value of this feeling. She began to express her ideas more freely and to be able to bring more of her talents and creativity into her workplace. Her ability to bring the changes and growth she experienced in therapy into the work community was a source of great pleasure to her. She felt she was making a truly important contribution there, which was also appreciated and valued by both her boss and her colleagues.

Some people are studying similar efforts on a larger scale. For example, Joyce Fletcher and others have brought this relational perspective to several research projects that have demonstrated the ways in which women often empower themselves and others in the work setting through engaging in growth-fostering relationships.[5] These women often facilitate teamwork, listen to and support other workers in getting the job done, and, like Phyllis, promote more mutual interactions among staff and administrators. What these researchers also found was that these contributions were not "seen" or acknowledged. Fletcher demonstrated how women's relational activities "got disappeared." No one saw how these women's "relational practices" contributed to the work itself, as well as to the community in the workplace. The findings from this project and others like it illustrate possible paths to counter the more individualistic and power-over strategies that characterize most of the settings in which we live and work.

An example of workers finding a way to create change in their work and in their lives on a larger scale is the Harvard Union of Clerical and Technical Workers (HUCTW) of the American Federation of State, County, and Municipal Employees (AFSCME).[6] The HUCTW was organized on the basis of building relationships among the workers. Workers came together to talk about their conditions and only after hard struggles was a contract with the management of the university finally won, a contract that contains many unusual relational and growth-fostering provisions. For example, the union won the right to create joint councils composed of workers and management throughout the university in every major work area. Through these councils, the workers (and members of management as well) have a mechanism for exerting ongoing influence on the conditions of their lives.

The union also has a vision of every worker's need to learn and grow and has created continuing opportunities for mutual support and learning through many forms of formal and informal teaching and learning groups. The union is committed to the belief that growth occurs in relationship, and in their relationships workers take on increasing knowledge and responsibility; this enlarges people's sense of themselves. Thus, the union has become a pathway — not only to better wages and working conditions, as important as these are — but also toward the expansion and fulfillment of the workers' whole lives.

We began by describing a perspective that originated at a very different point from other psychodynamic theories — not an attempt to account for pathology but rather an effort to describe healthy psychological development in women. We saw that the center of that development was connection — optimally, growth-fostering connection characterized by mutual empathy and mutual empowerment. We have tried to describe how this development can become derailed in the face of conditions that create disconnection and the loss of mutual empathy and empowerment. These conditions are inevitable in a society that is not yet based on mutuality; we all develop strategies for staying out of connection while needing and yearning for fuller connection.

This perspective creates a whole new attitude toward therapy and a new understanding of what it is to struggle with problems in life. It moves away from objectifying, hierarchical, pejorative ways of describing people and helps us to know how everybody comes into relationships carrying what we have called the relational paradox in some form. The only difference between patient and therapist is that it is the therapist's job to learn how to facilitate the movement in relationship toward more connection.

We believe that our focus on connection and disconnection speaks to the core of the human condition, the foundation that has remained obscure and out of focus. While all theories have spoken about relationships, this core has remained obscure because these theories emerged from an underlying preoccupation — though one not usually made explicit — with individual gratification and power. This preoccupation could arise only from the thinking of a group that has been the dominant group in society, and it inevitably reflects a distorted view of the total human condition. Once we examine more accurately the lives of all people — women *and* men — we find ourselves moving away from this preoccupation and toward a recognition of the necessity of human connection and the sources and consequences of disconnections.

APPENDIX

STONE CENTER WORKS IN PROGRESS

The following is a list of Works in Progress from the Stone Center at Wellesley College. (WP = Working Papers; AT = Audiotapes; VT = Video-tapes; PR = Project Reports.) For more information or to order copies of the Works in Progress, readers may contact Stone Center Publications at (617) 283–2510.

RELATIONAL DEVELOPMENT

Women and Empathy
Judith V. Jordan, Ph.D.; Janet L. Surrey, Ph.D.; Alexandra Kaplan, Ph.D.
   WP2

Women and Their Many Roles
Brunetta Wolfman, Ph.D.
   WP7

The Development of Women's Sense of Self
Jean Baker Miller, M.D.
   WP12

The "Self-in-Relation": A Theory of Women's Development
Janet L. Surrey, Ph.D.
   WP13

Empathy and Self Boundaries
Judith V. Jordan, Ph.D.
   WP16

Women's Self Development in Late Adolescence

Alexandra Kaplan, Ph.D.; Rona Klein, M.D.; Nancy Gleason, M.S.W.
   WP17

Feeling Like a Fraud
Peggy McIntosh, Ph.D.
   WP18

What Do We Mean by Relationships?
Jean Baker Miller, M.D.
   WP22

The Meaning of Mutuality
Judith V. Jordan, Ph.D.
   WP23

Clarity in Connection: Empathic Knowing, Desire, and Sexuality
Judith V. Jordan, Ph.D.
   WP29   AT E

Relationship and Empowerment
Janet L. Surrey, Ph.D.
   WP30

Connections, Disconnections, and Violations
Jean Baker Miller, M.D.
   WP33   AT G

Feeling Like a Fraud — Part II
Peggy McIntosh, Ph.D.
   WP37   AT I

*Relational Development: Therapeutic Implications of Empathy
   and Shame*
Judith V. Jordan, Ph.D.
   WP39   AT N

Empathy Revisited
Judith V. Jordan, Ph.D.; Alexandra Kaplan, Ph.D.; Janet L. Surrey, Ph.D.
   WP40   AT J

Courage in Connection
Judith V. Jordan, Ph.D.
   WP45   AT U

Alexandra Kaplan, Ph.D.
WP14

Women and Anger — Cultural Prohibitions and the Feminine Ideal
Teresa Bernardez, M.D.
WP31

From Depression to Sadness in Women's Psychotherapy
Irene P. Stiver, Ph.D.; Jean Baker Miller, M.D.
WP36   AT K

Relational Development: Therapeutic Implications of Empathy and Shame
Judith V. Jordan, Ph.D.
WP39   AT N

Revisioning Women's Anger: The Personal and the Global
Jean Baker Miller, M.D.; Janet L. Surrey, Ph.D.
WP43   AT T

Women and Suicide: The Cry for Connection
Alexandra Kaplan, Ph.D.; Rona Klein, M.D.
WP46   AT O

DIVERSITY

Women and Their Many Roles
Brunetta Wolfman, Ph.D.
WP7

Psychosocial Barriers to Black Women's Career Development
Clevonne Turner, M.S.W.
WP15

Understanding Black Single Parent Families: Stresses and Strengths
Michelene Malson, Ed.D.
WP25

Clinical Applications of the Stone Center Theoretical Approach to Minority Women

Clevonne Turner, M.S.W.
   WP28

*Alienation and Anger: A Black and a White Woman's Struggle
   for Mutuality in an Unjust World*
Katie G. Cannon, Ph.D.; Carter Heyward, Ph.D.
   WP54   AT Z

Cultural Diversity: Implications for Theory and Practice
Cynthia García Coll, Ph.D.
   WP59   AT A6

*Racial Identity Development and Relational Theory: The Case of
   Black Women in White Communities*
Beverly Daniel Tatum, Ph.D.
   WP63   AT A11

Building Connection Through Diversity
Cynthia García Coll, Ph.D.; Robin Cook-Nobles, Ed.D.; Janet L.
   Surrey, Ph.D.
   WP64   AT A13

Women, Race and Racism: A Dialogue in Black and White
Andrea Ayvazian, Ph.D.; Beverly Daniel Tatum, Ph.D.
   WP68

*The Experience of Migration: A Relational Approach in
   Therapy*
Margarita Alvarez, Ph.D.
   WP71   AT A21

Consciousness of Context in Relational Couples Therapy
Pamela Geib, Ed.D.; Marsha Pravder Mirkin, Ph.D.
   WP73   AT A20

Diversity at the Core: Implications for Relational Theory
Cynthia García Coll, Ph.D.; Robin Cook-Nobles, Ed.D.; Janet L.
   Surrey, Ph.D.
   WP75   AT A23

*Outside the Circle? The Relational Implications for White
   Women Working Against Racism*

Beverly Daniel Tatum, Ph.D.; Elizabeth Garrick Knaplund, M.A.
WP78

FAMILY RELATIONSHIPS / ADOLESCENTS / CHILDREN

Eating Patterns as a Reflection of Women's Development
Janet L. Surrey, Ph.D.
WP9

Women's Self Development in Late Adolescence
Alexandra Kaplan, Ph.D.; Rona Klein, M.D.; Nancy Gleason, M.S.W.
WP17

The Mother-Infant Tie: 50 Years of Theory, Science, and Science Fiction
Beverly Birns, Ph.D.
WP21

Beyond the Oedipus Complex: Mothers and Daughters
Irene P. Stiver, Ph.D.
WP26   AT A

Clarity in Connection: Empathic Knowing, Desire and Sexuality
Judith V. Jordan, Ph.D.
WP29   AT E

Reworking the Relationship: College Students and Their Divorcing Parents
Katherine Stone Kaufmann, M.S.W., Ed.D.
WP34   AT H

Dysfunctional Families and Wounded Relationships — Part I
Irene P. Stiver, Ph.D.
WP41   AT P

Dysfunctional Families and Wounded Relationships — Part II
Irene P. Stiver, Ph.D.
WP44   AT R

The Mother-Daughter Relationship: Themes in Psychotherapy

Pamela Geib, Ed.D.; Marsha Pravder Mirkin, Ph.D.
WP73   AT A20

LESBIAN RELATIONSHIPS

Issues in Psychotherapy with Lesbian Women
Nanette Gartrell, M.D.
WP10

*Coming Home to Self, Going Home to Parents: Lesbian Identity
Disclosure*
Lennie Kleinberg, Ed.D.
WP24

*Coming Out and Relational Empowerment: A Lesbian Feminist
Theological Perspective*
Carter Heyward, Ph.D.
WP38   AT M

*Intimacy in Lesbian Relationships: A Critical Re-Examination of
Fusion*
Julie Mencher, M.S.W.
WP42   AT S

On the Integration of Sexuality: Lesbians and Their Mothers
Wendy B. Rosen, Ph.D.
WP56   AT A5

*The Conundrum of Mutuality in Psychotherapy: A Lesbian
Dialogue*
Natalie S. Eldridge, Ph.D.; Julie Mencher, M.S.W.; Suzanne Slater,
M.S.W.
WP62   AT A14

Lesbians and Generativity: Not Everyone Waits for Midlife
Suzanne Slater, M.S.W.
WP72   AT A22

Questions and Controversies in Working with Lesbian Clients

Natalie Eldridge, Ph.D.; Julie Mencher, M.S.W.; Wendy Rosen, Ph.D.;
Suzanne Slater, M.S.W.
AT A28

POWER / EFFECTIVENESS

Women and Power: Some Psychological Dimensions
Jean Baker Miller, M.D.
WPI

Work Inhibitions in Women: Clinical Considerations
Irene P. Stiver, Ph.D.
WP3

Feeling Like a Fraud
Peggy McIntosh, Ph.D.
WPI8

Growing Up Intellectually: Issues for College Women
Blythe Clinchy, Ph.D.; Claire Zimmerman, Ph.D.
WPI9

Relationship and Empowerment
Janet L. Surrey, Ph.D.
WP30

Feeling Like a Fraud — Part II
Peggy McIntosh, Ph.D.
WP37   AT I

The Movement of Mutuality and Power
Judith V. Jordan, Ph.D.
WP53

Relational Theory in the Workplace
Joyce K. Fletcher, D.B.A.
WP77

SUBSTANCE ABUSE

Women, Addiction, and Codependency
Jean Kilbourne, Ed.D.; Janet L. Surrey, Ph.D.
AT A1

*Women and Prevention: Lessons from an Alcohol Education
    Program for College Women*
Nancy A. Gleason, M.S.W.
PR 3

VIDEOTAPES AND MANUALS OF PROJECT WAIT
(WELLESLEY AWARENESS IMPROV THEATER)

To Your Good Health: Women and Drinking
vt 1

The Inner Struggle: Women and Substance Abuse
vt 2

Putting It Together: Using Improvisational Theater in Prevention
vt 3

THERAPEUTIC APPLICATIONS

Female or Male Therapists for Women: New Formulations
Alexandra Kaplan, Ph.D.
WP5

The Meaning of Care: Reframing Treatment Models
Irene P. Stiver, Ph.D.
WP20

*Putting Theory into Practice: Creating Mental Health Programs
    for Women*
Nicolina Fedele, Ph.D.; Jean Baker Miller, M.D.
WP32   AT B

Dichotomous Thought and Relational Processes in Therapy

Alexandra Kaplan, Ph.D.
   WP35   AT D

Relational Development: Therapeutic Implications of Empathy and Shame
Judith V. Jordan, Ph.D.
   WP39   AT N

Women's Groups: How Connections Heal
Nicolina Fedele, Ph.D.; Elizabeth Harrington, Ph.D.
   WP47   AT Q

A Relational Reframing of Therapy
Jean Baker Miller, M.D.; Irene P. Stiver, Ph.D.
   WP52   AT A3

A Relational Approach to Therapeutic Impasses
Irene P. Stiver, Ph.D.
   WP58   AT A9

Movement in Therapy: Honoring the "Strategies of Disconnection"
Jean Baker Miller, M.D.; Irene P. Stiver, Ph.D.
   WP65   AT A16

Couples Therapy: A Relational Approach
Stephen J. Bergman, M.D., Ph.D.; Janet L. Surrey, Ph.D.
   WP66   AT A18

Relationships in Groups: Connection, Resonance and Paradox
Nicolina Fedele, Ph.D.
   WP69   AT A17

Relational Images and Their Meanings in Psychotherapy
Jean Baker Miller, M.D.; Irene P. Stiver, Ph.D.
   WP74   AT A25

Mutuality in Therapy: Ethics, Power and Psychology
Carter Heyward, Ph.D.; Judith V. Jordan, Ph.D.
   AT A7

Complexities and Dilemmas in Relational Psychotherapy
Judith V. Jordan, Ph.D.; Jean Baker Miller, M.D.; Irene P. Stiver, Ph.D.; Janet L. Surrey, Ph.D.
   AT A26

VIOLENCE / SEXUAL ABUSE

Annie G. Rogers, Ph.D.
   WP61   AT A12

Exiled Voices: Dissociation and the "Return of the Repressed" in Women's Narratives
Annie G. Rogers, Ph.D.
   WP67

Sexual Abuse of Patients by Psychiatrists
Nanette Gartrell, M.D.; Judith Lewis Herman, M.D.
   AT C

NOTES

INTRODUCTION

1. This educational program was consolidated when the Jean Baker Miller Training Institute was established in 1996. The four members of the theory group were its founding scholars. This institute offers clinicians training in our therapeutic approach and is applying this relational model in other areas, such as the workplace, schools, and other institutions.
2. For a list of the Stone Center publications, see the appendix.
3. See Judith Jordan, Alexandra Kaplan, Jean Baker Miller, Irene Stiver, and Janet Surrey, *Women's Growth in Connection* (New York: Guilford Press, 1991); and Judith Jordan, ed., *Women's Growth in Diversity* (New York: Guilford Press, 1997).
4. Although we are not completely comfortable with some of the connotations of the word "patient," we have found no satisfactory alternative. (See note 1, Chapter 7, for a more complete discussion of this issue.)

CHAPTER I
Relationships Revisited

1. Jean Baker Miller, *Toward a New Psychology of Women,* 2nd ed. (Boston: Beacon Press, 1986), 83.
2. Jean Baker Miller, "Connections, Disconnections, and Violations" *Work in Progress,* No. 33 (Wellesley, Mass.: Stone Center Working Paper Series, 1988), 2.
3. Ibid., p. 2.
4. See, for example, Judith Jordan, ed., *Women's Growth in Diversity* (New York: Guilford Press, 1997).
5. Martha Freeman, ed., *Always, Rachel: The Letters of Rachel Carson and*

Dorothy Freeman, 1952–1964: An Intimate Portrait of a Remarkable Friendship (Boston: Beacon Press, 1995), 20; 334, 336.

6. Miller, *Toward a New Psychology of Women,* 25–26.

7. See Judith Jordan, Alexandra Kaplan, Jean Baker Miller, Irene Stiver, and Janet Surrey, *Women's Growth in Connection* (New York: Guilford Press, 1991), and the list of Stone Center Working Papers in the appendix.

8. Carol Gilligan, "In a Different Voice: Women's Conception of Self and of Morality," *Harvard Educational Review* 47 (1977): 481–517; and *In a Different Voice* (Cambridge, Mass.: Harvard University Press, 1982).

9. See, for example, Carol Gilligan, "Joining the Resistance: Psychology, Politics, Girls and Women," *Michigan Quarterly Review* 29 (1990): 501–36; Lyn Mikel Brown and Carol Gilligan, *Meeting at the Crossroads* (Cambridge, Mass.: Harvard University Press, 1992).

10. Nancy Chodorow, *The Reproduction of Mothering* (Berkeley: University of California Press, 1978).

11. Mary Belenky, Blythe Clinchy, Nancy Goldberger, and Jill Tarule, *Women's Ways of Knowing* (New York: Basic Books, 1986).

12. We've been influenced by many works on women's experience. Please see Suggested Readings.

13. Examples of writings by earlier relational theorists are W. D.R. Fairbairn, *An Object Relations Theory of Personality* (New York: Basic Books, 1952); Harry Guntrip, *Psychoanalytic Theory, Therapy, and the Self* (New York: Basic Books, 1971); Karen Horney, *Neurosis and Human Growth* (New York: W. W. Norton, 1950); Howard Kirschenbaum and Valerie Henderson, eds., *The Carl Rogers Reader* (Boston: Houghton Mifflin, 1989); Harry Stack Sullivan, *The Interpersonal Theory of Psychiatry* (New York: W. W. Norton, 1953); Donald W. Winnicott, *The Maturational Process and the Facilitating Environment* (New York: International Universities Press, 1958).

14. Examples are: D. W. Detrick and S. P. Detrick, *Self Psychology: Comparisons and Contrasts* (Hillsdale, N.J.: The Analytic Press, 1989); Heinz Kohut, *The Analysis of the Self* (New York: International Universities Press, 1971); Robert Stolorow and George Atwood, *Contexts of Being: The Intersubjective Foundations of Psychological Life* (Hillsdale, N.J.: The Analytic Press, 1992); Steven Mitchell, *Relational Concepts in Psychoanalysis: An Integration* (Cambridge, Mass.: Harvard University Press, 1988). For a recent account of the work of many of the relational theorists at the New York University's Postdoctoral Program in Psy-

chotherapy and Psychoanalysis, see Lewis Aron, *A Meeting of the Minds: Mutuality in Psychoanalysis* (Hillsdale, N.J.: The Analytic Press, 1996).

CHAPTER II
How Do Connections Lead to Growth?

1. See Janet Surrey, "The 'Self-in-Relation': A Theory of Women's Psychological Development," in Judith Jordan, Alexandra Kaplan, Jean Baker Miller, Irene Stiver, and Janet Surrey, *Women's Growth in Connection* (New York: Guilford Press, 1991).

2. This separation of thought and feeling seems clearly linked to a long-standing gender division in Western culture. Thinking has been linked with men and is the valued capacity; feeling has been linked with women and is disparaged. In contrast, we believe that all thoughts are accompanied by emotions and all emotions have a thought content. Attempting to focus on one to the neglect of the other diminishes people's ability to understand and act on their experience. In this example, Tom is trying to act without feelings and Ann and Beth illustrate the fuller understanding and ability to act that follows from the attempt to integrate thinking and feeling.

3. Mutual empathy and mutual empowerment are concepts developed by our colleagues, Judith Jordan and Janet Surrey. They are basic to our whole understanding of relational psychology and also to our notions about psychotherapy. See the chapters by Judith Jordan and Janet Surrey in Jordan *et al.*, *Women's Growth in Connection*.

4. See chapters by Jordan and Surrey in Jordan *et al., Women's Growth in Connection*.

5. Past psychodynamic writers have talked about these inner creations mainly as introjects or internalized objects, usually of significant people or parts of people. (People are called "objects" in most traditional psychoanalytic theories.) Thus, infants and children are said to introject the "good object" or "good mother," the "bad mother," and the "good breast" or the "bad breast." We think people form more complicated internal images of more complex relational patternings. Over the years they change and elaborate on these images. Our notion is similar to, but not identical with, the concept of internal working

models proposed by John Bowlby in his studies on attachment. See John Bowlby, *Attachment and Loss,* vols. 1, 2, 3 (New York: Basic Books, 1969, 1973, 1980).

CHAPTER III
A Paradigm Shift

1. See chapters by Judith Jordan in Judith Jordan, Alexandra Kaplan, Jean Baker Miller, Irene Stiver, and Janet Surrey, *Women's Growth in Connection* (New York: Guilford Press, 1991).
2. Heinz Kohut, *The Analysis of the Self* (New York: International Universities Press, 1971).
3. See chapters by Judith Jordan and Janet Surrey in Jordan *et al., Women's Growth in Connection.*
4. Janet Surrey, "What Do You Mean by Mutuality in Therapy?" in Jean Baker Miller, Judith Jordan, Alexandra Kaplan, Irene Stiver, and Janet Surrey, "Some Misconceptions and Reconceptions of a Relational Approach," *Work in Progress,* No. 49 (Wellesley, Mass.: Stone Center Working Paper Series, 1991), 10. As a further explanation, Surrey adds, "We have moved away from prior views of separate selves connected in momentary cognitive-affective lapses (that is, empathy). Relationships are not seen as supports to individual development via unidirectional empathy and buttressing 'self-objects' but rather as goals in themselves, *arenas of growth and learning.*"
5. Janet Surrey, "The 'Self-in-Relation': A Theory of Women's Development," in Jordan *et al., Women's Growth in Connection.*
6. Alexandra Kaplan, "The 'Self-in-Relation': Implications for Depression in Women," in Jordan *et al., Women's Growth in Connection.*
7. W. D. R. Fairbairn, *An Object-Relations Theory of Personality* (New York: Basic Books, 1952).
8. For example, see Beatrice Beebe and Frank M. Lachman, "The Contribution of Mother–Infant Mutual Influence to the Origins of Self and Object Representation," *Psychoanalytic Psychology* 5 (1988): 305–37; Edward Tronick and Andrew Gianino, "Interactive Mismatch and Repair: Challenges to the Coping Infant," *Zero to Three* 6 (February, 1986): 1–6; Edward Tronick, "Emotions and Emotional Communication in the Infant," *American Psychologist* 44 (1989): 112–19. For an

account of much of this work by many authors see Daniel Stern, *The Interpersonal World of the Infant* (New York: Basic Books, 1985).

9. See, for example, Jean L. Chin *et al.*, *Diversity in Psychotherapy: The Politics of Race, Gender, and Ethnicity* (Westport, Conn.: Praeger, 1993); Lillian Cornas-Diaz and Beverly Greene, eds., *Women of Color* (New York: Guilford Press, 1994); bell hooks, *Feminist Theory: From Margin to Center* (Boston: South End Press, 1984); bell hooks, *Talking Back: Thinking Feminist, Thinking Black* (Boston: South End Press, 1989); bell hooks, *Sisters of the Yam: Black Women and Self-Recovery* (Boston: South End Press, 1993); Audre Lorde, *Sister Outsider: Essays and Speeches* (Trumansburg, N.Y.: Crossing Press, 1984); Elaine Pinder-hughes, *Understanding Race, Ethnicity, and Power* (New York: Guilford Press, 1989).

10. Surrey, "What Do You Mean by Mutuality in Therapy?", 10.

11. Alexandra Kaplan, Rona Klein, and Nancy Gleason, "Women's Self Development in Late Adolescence," in Jordan *et al.*, *Women's Growth in Connection.*

12. Niki Fedele, personal communication.

13. Jean Baker Miller, *Toward A New Psychology of Women,* 2nd ed. (Boston: Beacon Press, 1986).

14. In the psychodynamic field, the term "intrapsychic" tends to be used to refer to the internal contents of the mind as compared to more external and observable actions and behavior.

15. Judith Jordan, "Do You Believe that the Concepts of Self and Autonomy Are Useful in Understanding Women?" in Miller *et al.*, "Some Misconceptions and Reconceptions of a Relational Approach," 5.

16. Ibid.

17. Judith Jordan, "The Movement of Mutuality and Power," *Work in Progress,* No. 53 (Wellesley, Mass.: Stone Center Working Paper Series, 1991).

18. For a recent account of the effects of sexual and physical trauma, see Judith Herman, *Trauma and Recovery* (New York: Basic Books, 1993).

19. Many feminists have now provided a larger understanding of mothering and incisive critiques of mother-blaming. See, for example, Adrienne Rich, *Of Woman Born* (New York: Bantam Books, 1976); Paula Caplan, *Don't Blame Mother* (New York: Harper and Row, 1989); Beverly Birns, "The Mother-Infant Tie: Fifty Years of Theory, Science, and Science Fiction," *Work in Progress,* No. 21 (Wellesley, Mass.: Stone Center Working Paper Series, 1985); and Beverly Burns

and Dale F. Hay, eds., *The Different Faces of Motherhood* (New York: Plenum Press, 1988).

20. See, for example, Judith Herman, J. C. Perry, and Bessel van der Kolk, "Childhood Trauma in Borderline Personality Disorder," *American Journal of Psychiatry* 146 (1989): 490–95; and Jeffrey Bryer, Bernadette Nelson, Jean Baker Miller, and Pamela Krol, "Childhood Sexual and Physical Abuse as Factors in Adult Psychiatric Illness," *American Journal of Psychiatry* 144 (1987): 1426–30.

21. Eleanor Saunders and Frances Arnold, "Borderline Personality Disorder and Childhood Abuse: Revisions in Clinical Thinking and Treatment Approach," *Work in Progress,* No. 51 (Wellesley, Mass.: Stone Center Working Paper Series, 1991).

22. Carol Gilligan, "Joining the Resistance: Psychology, Politics, Girls and Women," *Michigan Quarterly Review* 29 (1990): 501–36.

CHAPTER IV
The Source of Psychological Problems

1. For an account of this work, see Daniel Stern, *The Interpersonal World of the Infant* (New York: Basic Books, 1985).

2. Janet Surrey, personal communication.

3. By contrast with concepts used in more traditional systems, such as "projective identification," this process is much more common and important. If we were to use more traditional terminology, we might call it something like "introjective relational identification," to mean that the individual takes into herself a problem that is relational or that in large part originates in the other person when that other person is an abuser or even merely unresponsive to what is occurring in the relationship. This process is always much more likely to occur when one person has more power to determine what can happen in the relationship.

4. For a discussion of a relational view in which anger can be seen as a resource, see Jean Baker Miller and Janet Surrey, "Revisioning Women's Anger: The Personal and the Global," *Work in Progress*, No. 43 (Wellesley, Mass.: Stone Center Working Paper Series, 1990).

5. Stern, *The Interpersonal World of the Infant.*

6. Irene Stiver and Jean Baker Miller, "From Depression to Sadness in

Women's Psychotherapy," *Work in Progress*, No. 36 (Wellesley, Mass.: Stone Center Working Paper Series, 1988).

7. Carolyn Swift, "Women and Violence: Breaking the Connection," *Work in Progress*, No. 27 (Wellesley, Mass.: Stone Center Working Paper Series, 1986).

8. Carol Gilligan, "Joining the Resistance: Psychology, Politics, Girls and Women," *Michigan Quarterly Review* 29 (1990): 501–36.

9. W. D. R. Fairbairn, *An Object Relations Theory of Personality* (New York: Basic Books, 1952); Karen Horney, *Neurosis and Human Growth* (New York: W. W. Norton, 1950); Heinz Kohut, *The Analysis of the Self* (New York: International Universities Press, 1971); Howard Kirschenbaum and Valerie Henderson, eds., *The Carl Rogers Reader* (Boston: Houghton Mifflin, 1989); Harry Stack Sullivan, *The Interpersonal Theory of Psychiatry* (New York: W. W. Norton, 1953).

CHAPTER V
How Disconnections Happen in Families

1. Judith Herman, "Father-Daughter Incest," in F. M. Ochberg, ed., *Post-Traumatic Therapy and Victims of Violence* (New York: Brunner / Mazel, 1988), 175–95.

2. K. F. Hays, "The Conspiracy of Silence Revisited: Group Therapy with Adult Survivors of Incest," *Journal of Group Psychotherapy, Psychodrama, and Sociometry* 39, 4 (1987): 148.

3. M. Cork, *The Forgotten Children* (Toronto: Paperjacks, Addiction Research Foundation, 1974), 32.

4. H. Epstein, *Children of the Holocaust* (New York: G. P. Putnam & Sons, 1979), 39.

5. Ibid., 209.

6. Janet Surrey, "The 'Self-in-Relation': A Theory of Women's Development," *Work in Progress*, No. 13 (Wellesley, Mass.: Stone Center Working Paper Series, 1984), 23.

7. N. Auerhahn and E. Prelinger, "Repetition in the Concentration Camp Survivor and Her Child," *International Review of Psychoanalysis* 10 (1983): 31–46.

8. E. Werner, "High-Risk Children in Young Adulthood: A Longitudi-

nal Study from Birth to 32 Years," *American Journal of Orthopsychiatry* 59 (1989): 72–81, 73.

9. Ibid., 73.

CHAPTER VI
Seeking Connection by Staying Out of Connection

1. V. Rachel, *Life Stories of Adult Children of Alcoholics* (San Francisco: Harper & Row, 1987), 39.

2. Ibid., 11.

3. E. Bass and E. Davis, *The Courage to Heal* (New York: Harper & Row, 1988), 45.

4. Ibid., 197.

5. D. Treadway, *Before It's Too Late* (New York: W. W. Norton, 1988), 202.

6. Sigmund Freud, "Beyond the Pleasure Principle," in *The Standard Edition of the Complete Psychological Works of Sigmund Freud*, ed. and trans. J. Strachey, vol. 1 (London: Hogarth Press, 1955), 7–64.

7. Treadway, *Before It's Too Late*.

8. N. Auerhahn and E. Prelinger, "Repetition in the Concentration Camp Survivor and Her Child," *International Review of Psychoanalysis* 10 (1983): 31–46.

CHAPTER VII
A Relational Reframing of Therapy

1. We do not like to use the word "patient." In our culture, it has often been used in a derogatory and distancing way. In its origins, however, it means one who suffers. Some prefer the word "client." We find that "client" has connotations of a business transaction. In fact, we have not been able to find a fully respectful word to describe a person who is in a relationship as a "helpee." We have decided to use the word "patient" as the best among bad choices.

2. This understanding of how Clara carried two levels of relational images is in sharp contrast to the more traditional views, which might interpret this observation as an indication of splitting. According to this view, "splitting" refers to the inability to integrate positive and nega-

tive "introjects" of parents (i.e., mother) and leads to a person shifting from extremes of idealization to denigration of the same person. It is considered to be a sign of a more primitive level of defense, indicating an inadequate resolution of early developmental stages.

3. Some authors have talked about parts of these points in other terms. For example, they write that therapists should be able to identify with the various introjects a person has taken in (and which she may also project onto the therapist) and should sense how the person feels in relation to each of these introjects. Instead, we think of this as being able to be empathic with the patient's internal relational images, images that are more complex than can be covered by a term like "introject." We also stress the two sides of the picture, that is, that the person is struggling to be in connection in the face of past relational images that militate against it.

4. As we said, we believe that these moments of moving into greater connection are the "levers" of movement, or change, in therapy. Most therapists know that they can make all the interpretations in the world and have nothing change. Many have said that the affective level has to be added. Others, depending on their theoretical outlook, add other concepts. For example, Kohutians will say that the therapist has to respond to the "selfobject" needs at the right level. We believe it is not a question of the affective level or selfobject needs only; it is feeling moved in the relationship, the kind of experience in which patient and therapist feel that they are moving to become more connected. We can't know these moments beforehand; we have to discover them with each person by working together.

5. Carol Gilligan, "Joining the Resistance: Psychology, Politics, Girls and Women," *Michigan Quarterly* 29 (1990): 501–36.

6. Judith Jordan, "Relational Development: Therapeutic Implications of Empathy and Shame," *Work in Progress*, No. 39 (Wellesley, Mass.: Stone Center Working Paper Series, 1989).

7. We want to make clear that we are not talking about any sort of quest for some ecstatic experience or emotional high. Nor are we talking about gratification of the therapist in the usual sense of that term. We are talking about the therapist *participating* in the relationship in a way that leads to mutual empathy and mutual empowerment. If both therapist and patient participate in this way they will inevitably move toward a sense of increased connection. We don't see how it could be otherwise.

8. Judith Jordan, "Empathy, Mutuality, and Therapeutic Change," in Judith Jordan, Alexandra Kaplan, Jean Baker Miller, Irene Stiver, and Janet Surrey, *Women's Growth in Connection* (New York: Guilford Press, 1991), 284.

CHAPTER VIII
Changing Traditional Psychotherapy Concepts

1. Traditional models of therapy protect the therapist from exposing her vulnerability and support her strategies of staying out of connection. For example, the emphasis on the therapist's objectivity and neutrality allows her to keep distance both from the patient and from her own feelings. Presumably the therapist's ability to help the patient is eroded when the therapist is too open to feel the patient's pain, or when she is deeply moved by this pain and the courage it takes to express it. This behavior has been labeled as the therapist's "over-involvement" with the patient, with the danger of a "loss of boundaries" which, in turn, leads to negative therapeutic effects, particularly regression. We find the opposite is true. As we've said, when the therapist is moved by the patient this creates the movement in therapy. It is not "over-involvement"; it is participation. And again, feeling does not preclude thinking; instead, lack of responsive feelings can preclude clear thinking.

   Judith Jordan has noted that for some people the therapist's neutrality can create intense anxiety because they will assume that this relationship is the *same* as those in the past, that is, unresponsive and then possibly also hurtful, disappointing, violating, and the like. A person may then still struggle to make connection with the therapist but in more desperate ways, often in nonrelational or maladaptive forms, sometimes labeled manipulative or acting out (Judith Jordan, "Challenges to Connection," *Work in Progress*, No. 60 [Wellesley, Mass.: Stone Center Working Paper Series, 1993]).

2. Sigmund Freud, "The Future Prospects of Psychoanalytic Therapy," in *The Standard Edition of the Complete Psychological Works of Sigmund Freud*, ed. and trans. J. Strachey, vol. 2 (London: Hogarth Press, 1957), 139–52.

3. H. Racker, *Transference and Countertransference* (New York: International Universities Press, 1953); P. Heimann, "On Countertransfer-

ence," *International Journal of Psychoanalysis* 31 (1950): 42–53; M. Little, "Countertransference and the Patient's Response to It," *International Journal of Psychoanalysis* 32 (1951): 30–40; D. Winnicott, "Hate in the Countertransference," *International Journal of Psychoanalysis* 30 (1949): 69–75.

4. See, for example, R. D. Stolorow, B. Bandchaft, and G. E. Atwood, *Psychoanalytic Treatment: An Intersubjective Approach* (Hillsdale, N.J.: Analytic Press, 1987); M. Gill, *Analysis of Transference*, vol. 1 (New York: International Universities Press, 1983).

5. In a paper on the treatment of eating disorders, Catherine Steiner-Adair offers a concept of countertransference which is most consonant with our perspective. In particular, she defines it as "the thoughts and feelings that take the therapist out of connection with the patient" (p. 233). See Catherine Steiner-Adair, "New Maps of Development, New Models of Therapy: The Psychology of Women and Treatment of Eating Disorders," in C. Johnson, ed., *Psychodynamic Treatment of Anorexia Nervosa and Bulimia* (New York: Guilford Press, 1991), 225–45.

6. Janet Surrey, "What Do You Mean by Mutuality in Therapy?" in Judith Jordan, Alexandra Kaplan, Jean Baker Miller, Irene Stiver, and Janet Surrey, "Some Misconceptions and Reconceptions of a Relational Approach," *Work in Progress*, No. 49 (Wellesley, Mass.: Stone Center Working Paper Series, 1991).

CHAPTER IX
Honoring the Strategies of Disconnection

1. Carol Gilligan, "Joining the Resistance: Psychology, Politics, Girls and Women," *Michigan Quarterly Review* 29 (1990): 501–36.

CHAPTER X
Joan's Story

1. Throughout this book we have drawn on examples from relatively long-term therapy. Longer therapies allow us the confidence that we understand people more fully. The current climate, however, which has led to limited therapy sessions, has obliged us to think seriously

about how to do relational therapy in this context. We have come to believe that knowledge gained from long-term therapy is extremely useful for short-term therapy. Indeed, we think a relational model is vital for short-term work.

2. Judith Jordan, "Relational Development: Therapeutic Implications of Empathy and Shame," *Work in Progress*, No. 39 (Wellesley, Mass.: Stone Center Working Paper Series, 1989).

CHAPTER XI
From Self to Community in Therapy, in Life

1. We have some differences with the formulations used by certain of these groups. An example is the codependency formulation. We see it as another form of blaming women for wanting relationships, rather than examining the nonmutuality of the relationships themselves. Obviously, too, we don't think the goal is to become "independent," and we believe that prospect can lead women to another form of self-blame if they don't achieve this goal. We know, however, that despite this criticism, some of these groups have been valuable for women; we think it is precisely because the women come together and form mutually empathic relationships with each other in the groups.

2. For any one of a variety of reasons, the therapist may lose her focus on responsiveness to the patient. If something has made her or the patient feel that she is out of connection, it is important that the patient and therapist examine this together, and especially important that the therapist acknowledge if she has been out of connection. If the therapist knows of factors that are interfering, she may explain them. Whether she does or not may vary depending on the situation. However, the recognition that she had failed to connect with the patient, and the discussion of this failure, are usually much more important than any particulars of her explanation.

3. Judith Jordan, "Relational Development: Therapeutic Implications of Empathy and Shame," *Work in Progress*, No. 39 (Wellesley, Mass.: Stone Center Working Paper Series, 1989).

4. Jean Baker Miller and Janet Surrey, "Revisioning Women's Anger: The Personal and the Global," *Work in Progress*, No. 43 (Wellesley, Mass.: Stone Center Working Paper Series, 1990).

5. Joyce Fletcher, "Relational Theory in the Workplace," *Work in Prog-*

ress, No. 77 (Wellesley, Mass.: Stone Center Working Paper Series, 1966).

6. Lisa Oppenheimer, "Women's Way of Organizing: A Conversation with AFSCME: Kris Rondeau and Gladys McKenzie," *Labor Research Review* 18, Fall–Winter (1991–92): 45–60; Susan Eaton, "The Customer Is Always Interesting: Unionized Harvard Clericals Renegotiate Work Relationships," in Cameron MacDonald and Carmen Sirianni, eds., *Work in the Service of Society* (Philadelphia: Temple University Press, 1996), 291–332.

SUGGESTED READINGS

These are some of the works about women's experience from which we've learned a great deal.

Bernardez, Teresa. "Women and Anger: Cultural Prohibitions and the Feminine Ideal," *Work in Progress* 31. Wellesley, Mass.: Stone Center Working Paper Series, 1988.

Boston Lesbian Psychologies Collective, eds. *Lesbian Psychologies: Explorations and Challenges.* Urbana, Ill.: University of Illinois Press, 1987.

Brown, Laura S., and M. P. P. Root, eds. *Diversity and Complexity in Feminist Therapy.* Binghamton, N.Y.: Harrington Press, 1990.

Brownmiller, Susan. *Against Our Will.* New York: Bantam, 1975.

Butler, Sandra. *Conspiracy of Silence.* San Francisco: Glide, 1976.

Caplan, Paula. *The Myth of Women's Masochism.* New York: E. P. Dutton, 1985.

———. *Don't Blame Mother: Mending the Mother-Daughter Relationship.* New York: Harper and Row, 1989.

Chesler, Phyllis. *Women and Madness.* New York: Avon, 1973.

Chin, Jean L., Victor De La Cancela, and Yvonne Jenkins. *Diversity in Psychotherapy: The Politics of Race, Gender, and Ethnicity.* Westport, Conn.: Praeger, 1993.

Cole, Johnnetta. *All American Women: Lines That Divide, Ties That Bind.* New York: Free Press, 1986.

Comas-Diaz, Lillian, and Beverly Greene, eds. *Women of Color.* New York: Guilford Press, 1994.

de Beauvoir, Simone. *The Second Sex.* New York: Vintage, 1952.

Dodson-Gray, Elizabeth. *Patriarchy as a Conceptual Trap.* Wellesley, Mass.: Roundtable Press, 1982.

Ehrenreich, Barbara, and Deirdre English. *For Her Own Good: 150 Years of Experts' Advice to Women.* Garden City, N.Y.: Anchor, 1979.

Eisler, Riane. *The Chalice and the Blade*. San Francisco: Harper and Row, 1987.

Fine, Michelle, and Adrienne Asch, eds. *Women with Disabilities: Essays in Psychology, Culture, and Politics*. Philadelphia: Temple University Press, 1988.

Goodrich, Thelma Jean, ed. *Women and Power: Perspectives for Therapy*. New York: W. W. Norton, 1991.

Harding, Sarah. *The Science Question in Feminism*. Ithaca, N.Y.: Cornell University Press, 1986.

Henley, Nancy. *Body Politics: Power, Sex, and Nonverbal Communication*. Englewood Cliffs, N.J.: Prentice-Hall, 1977.

Herman, Judith. *Trauma and Recovery*. New York: Basic Books, 1993.

Hochschild, Arlie R. *The Second Shift*. New York: Basic Books, 1989.

hooks, bell. *Feminist Theory: From Margin to Center*. Boston: South End Press, 1984.

———. *Talking Back: Thinking Feminist, Thinking Black*. Boston: South End Press, 1989.

———. *Sisters of the Yam: Black Women and Self-Recovery*. Boston: South End Press, 1993.

Ladner, Joyce. *Tomorrow's Tomorrow*. Garden City, N.Y.: Doubleday, 1971.

Lerner, Gerda. *The Creation of Patriarchy*. Oxford: Oxford University Press, 1986.

———. *The Creation of Feminist Consciousness*. Oxford: Oxford University Press, 1993.

Lerner, Harriet. *The Dance of Anger*. New York: Harper and Row, 1985.

———. *The Dance of Intimacy*. New York: Harper and Row, 1991.

———. *The Dance of Deception*. New York: HarperCollins, 1993.

Lorde, Audre. *Sister Outsider: Essays and Speeches*. Trumansburg, N.Y.: Crossing Press, 1984.

Lykes, M. Brinton. "Gender and Individualistic vs. Collectivist Bases for Notions about the Self," *Journal of Personality* 53 (1985): 357–83.

Martin, Del. *Battered Wives*. San Francisco: Glide, 1976.

McIntosh, Peggy. "Interactive Phases of Curricular Re-Vision: A Feminist Perspective," *Work in Progress* 124. Wellesley, Mass.: Stone Center Working Paper Series, 1983.

———. "White Privilege and Male Privilege: A Personal Account of Coming to See Correspondence through Work in Women's Studies," *Work in Progress* 189. Wellesley, Mass.: Stone Center Working Paper Series, 1988.

Morgan, Robin, ed. *Sisterhood Is Global*. Garden City, N.Y.: Anchor Press/ Doubleday, 1984.

Pinderhughes, Elaine. *Understanding Race, Ethnicity, and Power*. New York: Guilford Press, 1989.

Reiter, Rayna, ed. *Toward an Anthropology of Women*. New York: Monthly Review Press, 1975.

Rich, Adrienne. *On Lies, Secrets, and Silence*. New York: W. W. Norton, 1979.

———. *Of Woman Born: Motherhood as Experience and Institution*. New York: W. W. Norton, 1981.

———. "Compulsive Heterosexuality and Lesbian Experience," *Signs* 5 (1980): 631–60.

Tatum, Beverly Daniel. "Racial Identity Development and Relationship Theory: The Case of Black Women in White Communities," *Work in Progress* 63. Wellesley, Mass.: Stone Center Working Paper Series, 1994.

INDEX